ISLAM IN THE MODERN WORLD

Islam in the Modern World

Edited by

DENIS MacEOIN   AHMED AL—SHAHI

ST. MARTIN'S PRESS
New York

CONTENTS

PREFACE

The present collection of papers is based on a series of public lectures given in the University of Newcastle Upon Tyne in January, February and March 1982, under the auspices of the Public Lectures Committee of the University. The lectures were organized through the Department of Religious Studies, which had recently been enabled to establish a lectureship in Islamic Studies with funding from the Saudi Arabian Ministry of Higher Education. The aim of the series was to bring before a general audience certain aspects of modern Islam that are either unknown or misunderstood by many non-Muslims, if not by many Muslims as well. It was recognized from the beginning that we could not attempt to provide anything like a comprehensive introduction to the subject as a whole, but we did hope that the facets we were able to present would help members of the public to create in their own minds a rather broader picture of concepts and events than that normally available. There were, of course, a great many other topics on which we might have touched, but the limitations of time and resources forced us instead to single out a small number of themes connected to a number of central issues.

Following the completion of the series, it was decided to publish the orignal lectures together with one or two additional papers touching on similar themes. This is not primarily a book for scholars though scholars should find in it much of interest but for the general reader who already has a basic knowledge of Islam and wishes to expand and deepen it in respect of the modern situation. If it serves to make more familiar to the public at large certain neglected yet significant aspects of a much misunderstood subject, it will have fulfilled its purpose.

The system of transliteration used will be familiar to Islamicists. Unfortunately, the practicalities of setting the camera-ready copy on a word processor have meant that it has not been possible to incorporate either macrons or sub-linear dots in the main text, but these have been

Preface

supplied in the index. Well-known place and personal names
have usually been left in their popular form, while Turkish
words are given in their modern spelling. Raised 'c' (^{c})
indicates the letter ^{c}ayn, a harsh guttural consonant which
the beginner may convey by a glottal stop.

The editors wish to express their thanks to the Saudi
Arabian Ministry of Higher Education for financial help in the
publication of this collection; to John Sawyer for his advice
and assistance in the co-ordination of the funding; and to
Mrs. Hazel Moodie and her staff at Northumbrian Computer
Management, Newcastle, for their patient and efficient
handling of so much unfamiliar material

Denis MacEoin
Department of Religious Studies

Ahmed Al-Shahi
Department of Social Studies

University of Newcastle Upon Tyne

INTRODUCTION

In recent years, events in the Islamic world have
captured the attention of the general public in the West to an
unprecedented degree. Media coverage of these events --
central among which has been the Islamic revolution in Iran
-- has served to stimulate widespread interest in Islam as a
religion and a way of life, but, with few exceptions,
newspaper and television reports have tended to reinforce
existing prejudices or to confirm popular misconceptions -- a
point emphasized by Edward Said in his recent study,
Reporting Islam (1981). There are, of course, well-informed
journalists whose reports on the Islamic world are frequently
illuminating, but the problems of simplification and
stereotyping that beset the popular media in most areas are
greatly exacerbated here by the underlying ignorance of the
public at large concerning things Islamic, an ignorance which
extends to languages, geography, politics, history, religion,
art, music, and much else. Ignorance of things Islamic may
not, perhaps, be a whit inferior to ignorance of things
Russian, Chinese, Japanese, Hindu or Buddhist, but it is
still disproportionate to the importance of Islam in world
affairs and reflects a persistence of ethnocentric attitudes
which are sure to prove increasingly counter-productive
within a context of growing political and cultural
interdependence.

The perpetuation of stereotyped images is,
unfortunately, fostered not only by insular attitudes at home
but also by forms of revivalism abroad that all too often
conform to those images and thus enhance them in the
Western mind. The post-colonial attempt to find and assert an
identity rooted in Islamic consciousness and sustained by
Islamic values has led many Muslims to adopt and to advocate
precisely those attitudes and modes of action that correspond
most closely to the more extreme Western stereotypes: rigid
application of the religious law, fanaticism towards
non-believers, even advocacy of a holy war against secularism
and westernization or the 'Great Satan'. The positive

elements of the Islamic revival are, for many in the West, understandably veiled by the negative images of strident fundamentalism, obscurantism, religious chauvinism, and rejectionism. Outside the realm of the popular media, the situation is better but far from ideal. At the farther end of the spectrum, important advances have been made in the field of Islamic and Middle East studies (1), notably in the increasing concern of scholars with empirical data that often leads to conclusions radically different to those reached through prescriptive, text-based research. The application within the field as a whole of techniques and methods developed earlier by historians, economists, sociologists, anthropologists, and others and the gradual shift from amateurism and polymathism to a more specialized professionalism have led to important changes in perspective and direction. At the same time, the criticisms directed by Jacques Waardenburg, Edward Said and others (2) against 'orientalism' and, in particular, the charge that orientalists have been concerned less with empirical reality than with their own vision of what the Orient or Islam should be, have introduced new elements of doubt and self-questioning or defensiveness into the field. To the extent that criticisms of this kind are justified, such questioning can only be to the good, but there are serious dangers that, in rejecting the orientalist tradition outright, some modern scholars may discard much that was valuable along with the less desirable. This problem has been intensified by the readiness of many Muslim writers to adopt the anti-orientalist position uncritically as a device for the rejection of all Western studies on Islam, together with Western academic and scientific values. Such a response is less than helpful in a situation where increased understanding on both sides is more necessary than ever. Polemics do not usefully take the place of informed, rational debate.

Two contributions to the present collection examine from different viewpoints some of the questions raised by the encounter of the Islamic and Western worlds. William Watt is widely known and respected as an Anglican clergyman and academic who has shown himself capable of the most profound insights into historical and religious questions central to Islam. In his published work as an Islamicist, he has not lost sight of his own religious commitment and has constantly displayed a deep consciousness of the need for a widening dialogue between Christians and Muslims in the modern world; he himself has contributed regularly and crucially to the process of bridge-building between adherents of the two faiths. In his present paper, he has provided an historical outline of relations between Islam and the West as the background to contemporary problems and possibilities. His discussion of the present situation concentrates above all on the problems encountered by educated Muslims in the post-colonial period, confronting the Western world as a continuing threat on both the cultural and religious levels. The hazards posed for ecumenicism by the spread of Western-based secularism on the one hand and by a resurgent fundamentalist Islamic consciousness on the other are brought, in the final section, to the foreground of the discussion.

Brian Turner, until recently at the Department of Sociology in Aberdeen University, has established a reputation as a sociologist seriously interested in Islam and capable of bringing his expertise within his own subject to bear on misunderstoood or neglected aspects of Islamic religion or society. In 'Accounting for the Orient', he has sought to examine the problem of 'orientalism' within a broader sociological perspective, beginning with the theories of Eastern society developed by Weber and Marx (notably with respect to the problem of why capitalism emerged in Europe rather than the Orient) and continuing through an appraisal of Said's critique in terms of Michel Foucault's concept of 'discourse'.

In his concluding sentence, Professor Turner suggests that 'one solution to theological ethnocentrism ... would be to emphasize those points of contact and sameness which unite the Christian, Jewish and Islamic traditions into mere variations on a religious theme which in unison provide the bases of our culture'. John Sawyer's paper on 'Islam and Judaism' deals with the relatively unexplored area of Jewish Muslim relations and seeks to illustrate precisely those 'points of contact and sameness' which may prove most valuable as a means of overcoming theological ethnocentrism. Islamic relations with Christendom have been dominated by the political realities which were born with the spread of Islam and the beginnings of European resistance to it and the Empire it spawned. Until the modern period, however, with the exception of the Jewish Khazar state of the middle ages, Islam has confronted Judaism on a wholly different level. As a result, much less attention has been given to the question of relations between the two religions since the seventh century (and virtually none to more obscure areas such as Islamic-Samaritan relations). As a Biblical scholar specializing in Judaism who has also devoted much time to the study and teaching of Islam, Professor Sawyer has been able to examine the issue from both sides. By introducing into the subject of contemporary Jewish-Muslim relations issues dating back as far as the inception of Islam (such as the problem of the Prophet's treatment of the Jews), he has placed such questions as the Arab-Israeli conflict within a much wider context, both chronologically and imaginatively, than is usually provided.

One of the most enduring stereotypes of Islamic society

in the Western mind is that of the Muslim woman and her role in a male-dominated environment. In his paper on 'Islam and the Feminine', Ralph Austin has attempted to look behind the obvious issues of marriage and divorce legislation, the veil and seclusion systems, or modernist issues such as female suffrage, in order to penetrate more deeply and at a more abstract level to the forces shaping the role of women in Islamic society, both traditional and modern. Dr. Austin has sought to avoid the 'orientalist' trap of looking for 'typically Islamic' tendencies, not by means of a narrow series of case studies, but by seeking to locate wider concepts such as 'patriarchalism' or 'the feminine' within a broad Islamic context. His conclusions express the problems for modern Muslims in coming to terms with the new roles demanded by women, not in terms of electoral reform or legislation but with respect to deeply-laid psychological and cultural attitudes.

Perhaps the most crucial factor contributing to the creation and perpetuation of popular stereotypes is the tendency to present Islam as a monolithic entity both geographically and chronologically, with the Prophet, the Qur'an, the Sunna, possibly classical Sufism, and the culture of the early Islamic Empire as static points of reference even in discussions of modern Islam. No-one would deny that these and related matters are still of the most vital importance both in Islamic consciousness and reality, but it is clear that they do not form the totality of either. The Iranian revolution has helped bring home to many people in the West the importance of Shi^{c}ism as an alternative tradition within Islam largely neglected or undervalued in many standard accounts. But there remains a vast undercurrent of Islamic faith and practice in the modern world that goes unsuspected by most Westerners.

Three of the present papers are devoted to the study of Sufism in the contemporary Islamic world. The recrudescence of dogmatic versions of Islamic orthodoxy has in some ways served to obscure the persistence of alternative expressions of traditional religiosity, notably in the shape of the Sufi orders and in related forms of popular religion, such as saint-worship. Ernest Gellner has argued (3) that a scripturally-based, egalitarian, orthodox Islam is well suited to the demands of the modern world and that, by way of contrast, the popular, hierarchical, pluralist forms of religion are less able to adjust to changed conditions in contemporary society and may, indeed, be permanently eclipsed by more 'protestant' forms of the faith. There are, nevertheless, important possibilities for religious renewal in the more orthodox, urban forms of Sufism, and it is significant that, in some areas, the orders have continued to play a role in the life of society and even to enter the arena of modern politics.

In 'Sufism and Psuedo-Sufism', Laurence Elwell-Sutton

seeks to disentangle the classical tradition of Sufism as a specifically Islamic form of mystical experience from those modern Western movements that have claimed a Sufi lineage while attempting to cut themselves off from the heritage of Islamic faith and practice. By emphasizing the interdependence of Islam as an exoteric tradition and community on the one hand and Sufism as an esoteric intensification of its religious life on the other, Professor Elwell-Sutton has demonstrated the possibility of a renewal of Islamic values in the modern world based on principles wider than but not dismissive of the compulsion towards orthodoxy and orthopraxy that underlies present-day fundamentalism in Iran and other countries.

Ahmed Al-Shahi's paper on 'Sufism in Modern Sudan' illustrates the continuing role of Sufism and holy men in contemporary Islamic society by focussing attention on the activities of the Khatmiyya Order and its involvement in contemporary Sudanese political life. The roots of this nineteenth-century fraternity in traditional piety and mystical experience are provided as a background to its later development as a major force in Sudanese society in general and in the area of modern electoral politics in particular. Dr. Al-Shahi's wide first-hand experience of the topics with which he deals, combined with his training as an anthropoligist have enabled him to present a rounded picuture of an Islamic society balanced between traditional and modernizing forces.

John Norton's study of 'Bektashis in Turkey' deals with the problems of adjustment to secularized society faced by a much older and more overtly heterodox order, that of the Bektashiyya. Emphasizing the fact that 'Bektashi rejection of orthodoxy had always attracted many political dissidents to its (the order's) ranks', Mr. Norton examines the ways in which the order sought to cope with the prosciption of the Sufi fraternities in Turkey in 1925, and demonstrates how a stress on nationalist features has enabled its followers to find a niche in contemporary life, particularly through the emergence of what he terms 'political Bektashis'. Here again, extensive personal observation has served to add a note of authenticitiy to a knowledge of the texts.

Lack of understanding of the heterogeneity of Islamic society has resulted in a widespread tendency to treat all examples of Islamic resurgence as if they stemmed from the same causes and were directed towards identical ends. Although there is no question that most if not all movements of religious revival in the Islamic world share an antipathy towards Western values and are united in seeking to cultivate a religiously-determined identity, considerable ideological differences may, in fact, lurk behind the facade of simple revivalism. Such differences are most apparent between the proponents of Islamic revolution in Shi^{c}i Iran on the one hand and the leaders of fundementalist movements such as the

Introduction

Muslim Brothers in the Sunni world.

In his paper on 'The Shi^{c}i Establishment in Modern
Iran', Denis MacEoin seeks to trace the origins of the recent
revolution in the development of Twelver Shi^{c}ism during the
past two centuries. He is particularly concerned to illustrate
the significance of the intensification during this period of
charismatic authority within the religious institution,
culminating in the emergence of Ayatollah Khumaini as a
politically successful leader whose power is drawn from
primarily religious sources. This development of charismatic
leadership located in outstanding individuals is set within the
context of the routinization and rationalization of the religious
establishment as a whole and contrasted with the emergence of
novel forms of heterodoxy in nineteenth-century Iran. Dr.
MacEoin's paper acts in some measure as a corrective to a
particularly misleading journalistic stereotype of recent years
-- the portrayal of 'the mosque' as an institution comparable
to the Western 'church'.

Derek Hopwood's paper on 'A Movement of Renewal in
Islam' examines three extreme cases of religious reaction
against the pressures of modern society: the emergence of the
messianic sect that took control of the Great Mosque of Mecca
for a brief period in 1979, the unrelated messianic uprising
that occurred in Kano, Nigeria, in 1980, and the development
of the group responsible for the assassination of President
Sadat of Egypt in 1981. Dr. Hopwood sees in such movements
'part of what may be termed an Islamic response to change
forced upon societies unwilling to accept such change', but he
is at pains to emphasize his belief that the idea of a 'revival'
of Islam is in some ways misleading, not least because 'Islam
has been a permanent factor in the lives of believers for
centuries', even if this has only become apparent to many
Westerners quite recently. Here, as in other papers, the
continuity between past and present, tradition and
resurgence, runs as a constant thread through events and
ideas.

In spite of such reactions as those described by Dr.
Hopwood, the forces of modernism within the Islamic world
remain considerable, and many have recognized the necessity
and inevitability of adaptation to these forces. Such
adaptation is particularly inescapable in those areas of life
that bring Muslim states and peoples into direct and constant
contact with the non-Muslim world, such as international
politics, development, and trade. In 'Islam and Economic
Development', Rodney Wilson, like Bryan Turner a
non-Islamicist bringing important outside perspectives into the
field, seeks to outline the main problems associated with the
implementation of Islamic norms within the context of modern
economic activities. Dr. Wilson illustrates the ways in which
modern Muslims, having in the last decade abandoned earlier
attempts to reconcile Islam with either capitalism or socialism,

now seek to reassert traditional Islamic values in this area.
'What has occurred', he says, 'is an attempt to make economic
practice conform to these values, rather than any
re-interpretation of basic doctrine'. Examples are given of
ways in which Muslim economists have tried to tackle problems
relating to investment, banking, insurance, and related areas
likely to involve practices contrary to Islamic principles.
Less theoretical issues surround the subject of physical
development, and it is perhaps for that reason that relatively
little attention has been paid to the problems raised by
changes effected in the human environment by the
introduction of methods of building construction and urban
planning developed in another hemisphere. In 'Architecture in
the Islamic World', Miles Danby, whose own practical
experience as an architect in Islamic countries is
considerable, attempts to define the principal characteristics
of traditional architecture and town planning before tackling
the problems raised by urban expansion and the introduction
of modern techniques and materials.

NOTES

1. For a detailed survey of developments in this field up to
the modern period, see M. Rodinson 'The Western Image
and Western Studies of Islam' in J. Schacht and E. C.
Bosworth (eds.) The Legacy of Islam 2nd. ed. (Oxford,
1974).

2. Jacques Waardenburg' L'Islam dans le miroir de
l'Occident' (The Hague, 1963); Edward Said Orientalism
(New York, 1978).

3. Ernest Gellner Muslim Society (Cambridge, 1981), p.56
ff.

ISLAM IN THE MODERN WORLD

ISLAM AND THE WEST

W. Montgomery Watt

One of the features of our contemporary world is that personal friendships between Muslims and Christians have become possible and even frequent. More than a century ago when Sir William Muir in India was working on the life of Muhammad he was helped by an Indian scholar, but one has the impression that this did not develop into a personal friendship. Some of the great Islamists of the earlier part of this century had Muslim friends - Ignaz Goldziher, Sir Hamilton Gibb and above all Louis Massignon, who regarded his recovery of his Christian faith as due in large part to the faith of a Muslim friend. Other well-known Islamists of the same period, however, had few contacts with Muslims and worked almost exclusively from books. Since about 1950 this has largely changed. The Christian or Western scholar of today who wants to have Muslim friends has no difficulty in finding them, and they add an important perspective to his studies, for one has to speak respectfully of the religion of an esteemed friend. The few Western scholars who propound bizarre and improbable theories of the origin of Islam presumably have no Muslim friends.

When Muhammad and his followers first met Christians they were welcomed in friendly fashion, and some passages of the Qur'an reciprocate this friendly attitude. Before Muhammad's death, however, his armies were attacking Christian allies of the Byzantine Empire, and this led to some change of feeling on both sides. Even so, however, native Christians in Egypt welcomed the Muslim invaders as liberators from the Byzantine Greeks whom they hated. The Byzantines, of course, came to see in the Muslims powerful enemies who had wrested several provinces from them though they had been repulsed from Constantinople. By a century after Muhammad's death the Muslims had occupied most of Spain and were sending raiding parties into France. Even after the Christians of Western Europe had halted the Muslim advance they still saw Islam as a threat. The Muslims not only had great military power but were culturally at a higher

1

level. They also had an unshakeable conviction in the superiority of the Islamic religion.

In these circumstances it is not surprising that the Christians of Western Europe elaborated their intellectual 'defences' against Islam. This began in popular forms, but after the initial successes of the Christian Reconquista in Spain and the commencement of the Crusades, Christian scholars produced what can only be called a 'distorted image' of Islam. Among their allegations were that Islam was a religion which spread by the sword, that Muhammad was consciously an impostor, and that Muslims were encouraged to sexual laxity by the Qur'an. These allegations are definitely false. It is, of course, true that the Islamic state or empire spread by the sword, but the conquered Christians or Jews, far from being forced to become Muslims, became 'protected minorities' (dhimmis), following their own religion and having a degree of autonomy under their religious head. Again, sound historical method requires acceptance of the view that Muhammad was sincere in believing that he could distinguish the revelations sent him by God from his own thinking. The question of sexuality is difficult, but the most likely view is that in general the Qur'an was trying to bring about a stricter control of sexual practices.

It is important that the Christian of today should realize that this 'distorted image' has dominated most European and Western and Christian thinking until the later eighteenth century and even yet has not completely lost its influence. Nevertheless a more correct image of Islam has in great measure been attained, partly through the labours of scholars in acquiring fuller and more accurate information, and partly through the growing appreciation of Islamic achievements by poets and writers as well as scholars, not least the achievements in religious matters. This means in practice that, when a Christian today enters into dialogue with Muslims, he must do so on the basis of accepting Islam as a genuine religion and Muhammad as inspired by God. To suppose that Christians worship God and Muslims Allah and that the two are distinct is like distinguishing Dieu worshipped by Frenchmen from ho Theos worshipped by Greeks. Allah is simply the Arabic word for God, and is used by several million Arabic-speaking Christians. Again, the admission that Muhammad was genuinely inspired by God does not necessarily imply acceptance of all later Muslim assertions about the nature of the revelations he received.

The Muslims were at first friendly towards Christians, since certain Christians had given them encouragement and help. The Qur'an accepts Jesus as a prophet sent by God, and even has an account of his birth from a virgin, though this is interpreted by Muslims simply as a miracle, not as a sign that he is 'son of God', since they consider it impossible for God to have a son. The Qur'an also spoke of the revelation through Jesus as identical in essentials with that through Muhammad. Gradually, however, as Muslims became aware of differences between Biblical and Qur'anic teaching, the Qur'an had to bring them criticisms of Christian doctrine, especially of the doctrine of the Trinity. What was criticized here, however, was not the doctrine of One God in three hypostases but a doctrine of three gods. This last, of course, may well have been a popular misrepresentation of Christian belief current in Arabia even among Christians. On the basis of some verses in the Qur'an, which, taken at their face value, appear to deal with minor matters, later Muslim scholars elaborated a theory of the 'corruption' (tahrif) of the Jewish and Christian scriptures; and this proved a very effective 'defence' for Muslims when arguing against Christian opponents who might be more sophisticated, since it prevented the Christians arguing from Biblical texts.

The doctrine of the 'corruption' of the Bible fitted in well with an attitude which is deep-seated among Muslims and still affects their relationships with non-Muslims and with cultures other than the Islamic. The attitude may be illustrated by a story which is almost certainly not historically true but is yet significant. When in 642 the Muslims occupied Alexandria, the capital of Egypt and a leading centre of Hellenistic culture, they found the great library. The general in command wrote to the Caliph asking what was to be done with the books in the library and received the reply, 'If these books agree with the Qur'an, they are unnecessary and may be destroyed; if they disagree with the Qur'an, they are dangerous and should certainly be destroyed'. In other words, the Qur'an - and the Qur'an alone - has all the religious and moral truth required by all mankind until the Day of Judgement. In accordance with this feeling or assumption, Muslims have often avoided studying Christian, Western and other 'foreign' books, or have borrowed from them without admitting it (as happened with some Biblical materials). The one great acknowledged exception was the study of Greek science and philosophy. The Caliph al-Ma'mun (813-33) set up an institution for translating Greek works, and some Muslims eventually produced brilliant original work in medicine and philosophy; but these were always regarded as 'foreign sciences' which did not form part of Islamic higher education, and in recent centuries, especially among Sunnis, they have mostly been neglected.

One of the unfortunate consequences of this Muslim belief in the self-sufficiency of Islam and its superiority to the teaching of the 'Christian' West has been an educational cleavage in the Islamic world between traditional Islamic education and a European-type education. Traditional Islamic education began with village Qur'an-schools where boys, in the course of learning the Qur'an by heart, also learned to read and write, and had its summit in institutions like the thousand-year-old university of al-Azhar in Cairo. Those who controlled this system were unwilling to introduce 'foreign' disciplines as taught in Europe. In the first decade of the nineteenth century when Egypt was still a province of the Ottoman Empire, the Ottoman general in command there, Muhammad ^cAli, made himself an autonomous ruler, though still acknowledging the Ottoman Sultan as suzerain. One of his ambitions was to create an Egyptian army on the European model, and for this he required officers trained in various European disciplines not included in the traditional Islamic curriculum. Knowing the conservatism of the Islamic system, he made no attempt to widen it but simply imported European teachers for his officers. This was the initiation of a process which after about a century resulted in the existence in many Islamic countries of two seperate educational systems. Alongside the traditional one was a European-type system, ranging from primary and secondary schools to European-type universities. Some of these had been established by Christian missionaries, but many - eventually most - were created by Muslim rulers themselves when they realized that for their countries to exist as modern states they had to have education of this type. It was from such institutions that they drew the majority of their professional classes, civil servants, other office workers, and higher manual workers. By the second half of the twentieth century most of the education in the majority of Islamic countries was of this kind. An incidental drawback was that for long there was no formal religious education, since the official Islamic religious teachers, owing to their traditional training, were incapable of using the teaching methods normal in the modern schools.

This growth of European-type education had profound reverberations within Islamic society. The products of the modern system constituted a new class distinct from the old upper and lower classes, and this new class was anxious to have its share of power. In some cases army officers were in effect its representatives. At the same time the clerical class of religious scholars was greatly weakened. In Islam there are, strictly speaking, no clergymen, since there are no priests or pastors. Those called 'clergymen' in recent years by Western media are religious scholars, and they may be said to constitute a clerical class or 'religious institution'. The most general term for them is ^culama, 'men of knowledge' or 'scholars', and their expertise is primarily in the jurisprudence based on the shari^ca or 'Islamic law'. Shari^ca differs, however, from law as understood in the West, since it is a divinely-given ideal of conduct embracing every aspect of human life, personal, social, political and liturgical. Detailed rules have to be elaborated from a few basic principles contained in the Qur'an and in the example of Muhammad; and this elaboration is the province of qualified ^culama, since even the most autocratic Muslim ruler is not entitled to make laws. The work of elaboration is based on analogical reasoning and similar devices. Thus if the ^{c}ulama are asked whether the shari^{c}a permits the drinking of whisky, they will reply that it forbids it; their ground for saying this is that the Qur'an forbids the drinking of wine, that this is because wine is intoxicating, and that, since whisky is intoxicating, it falls under the same prohibition.

In the Ottoman Empire the religious institution was hierarchically organized, and up to about 1850 was extremely powerful. It controlled both the formulation of law and the application of law through the courts, and it also controlled all higher education. The growth in Islamic countries of European-type education over which the ^{c}ulama had no control was a serious erosion of their powers. At the same time they were losing their power in the sphere of law. By 1850 there was a large volume of commerce between the Ottoman Empire and Europe, but the ^{c}ulama were unwilling to adapt current practice to this novel situation by reconsidering how the basic principles of the shari^{c}a could be applied. Because of this refusal, the Ottoman Sultans began to publish 'codes' for particular aspects of legal practice, such as maritime commerce. At first these were ostensibly only administrative regulations for applying the shari^{c}a, and this was within the competence of the Sultan; but before long the codes became a partial alternative system of law for which a new type of law-court was required, in which traditional Islamic legal training was irrelevant. By 1950 in many Muslim countries the shari^{c}a was being applied only in questions of marriage, divorce and inheritance, and little else. Thus the religious institution had lost most of its influence, not merely in education but also in the sphere of law and the administration of justice.

This account of the religious institution as it is found, though with some variations, in all Muslim countries is clearly relevant to the revolution in Iran; but a balanced understanding of events there also requires some consideration of what is commonly called the Islamic revival or resurgence. This is a genuinely religious movement affecting both predominantly Islamic countries and those where Muslims are in a minority. It is essentially a response to the tremendous impact the West has had on Muslims everywhere. One of the aspects of this impact was the political, since as a result of colonialism many Muslims found themselves under non-Muslim rule. Another aspect was economic - the spread to Islamic countries of the products of Western technology. Muslims, especially wealthy Muslims, have usually welcomed these products because they made life more comfortable and luxurious. The acceptance of Western products, however, inevitably leads to social changes. Men and women have to be trained to use and repair cars, trains, aeroplanes, factory machinery, typewriters, hospital equipment, and so forth. It is such training that has necessitated the growth of the European-type educational system, while this system in turn, as already noted, has produced a new social class and disturbed the old balance of classes. Not surprisingly people feel unsettled and anxious because the social world they knew has disappeared. This is the situation out of which has come the Islamic resurgence.

The resurgence is a genuine movement of ordinary people who in their insecurity turn back to the old religion. Because so much in their daily lives has been westernized, they feel in danger of losing their identity as Muslims. As a consequence the resurgence is characterized by an emphasis on matters which reassert people's Islamic identity and their difference from the West, notably the prohibition of alcohol and usury, and the use of the veil by women. Some Muslims involved in the resurgence are aware of current social problems in their various countries, but this is not a concern of the resurgence as such.

Throughout the Islamic world, the members of the religious institution in each country share in the general feeling of insecurity and loss of identity, and experience something of the resurgence within themselves. As institutions, however, they are also aware of their own loss of power and influence. Since the establishment of the 1906 Constitution in Iran and the creation of Pakistan in 1948, the ^culama of these countries have urged on the statesmen that there should be a committee of ^culama to review parliamentary decisions and say whether they are in accordance with the shari^ca; but the statesmen, probably wisely, always rejected this view. In many countries, however, the ^culama have realized that there is a possibility of using the Islamic resurgence to recover power for themselves. That the Iranian religious institution has been conspicuously successful in this is due to various special factors. Iran is the only country where the Imami - Shi^ci form of Islam is the established religion, and this form makes the religious institution more independent of the ruler than in Sunni countries; in Iran they are ultimately responsible not to the actual ruler but to the 'hidden Imam', and they have sources of income not controlled by the ruler. In Iran too they have had a long tradition of resistance to oppressive or unsatisfactory governmental measures on behalf of the people. In autumn 1982 it appears that so far they have done better than might have been expected, but only the future will show if they are tackling the long-term problems.

While it seems unlikely that the ^culama in any Sunni country will attain the sort of political power now wielded by those in Iran, many are trying hard to recover some of their power in the educational sphere. In 1977 the First World Congress on Muslim Education was held in Mecca and was attended by ^culama from many countries. The participants were fully aware of the danger to the traditional Islamic way of life arising from the fact that a high percentage of Muslim youth receives a Western-type education and nothing apart from it. They passed a recommendation that Muslim scholars should be called on to work out Islamic foundations for all the sciences, natural, social and humanistic; and they seemed to think that this could be achieved by providing an adequate number of research posts. They thus show themselves to be dominated still by the belief in the self-sufficiency of Islam, and they fail·to realize that their programme requires that they themselves develop some appreciation of the positive achievements of the West in subjects like philosophy and theology as well as in the sciences. There is also little realization among most of the ^{c}ulama of the vast amount of work to be done if the shari^{c}a is to be applied in modern states. The problem is not so much one of introducing changes in detailed rules as in answering novel questions, such as: What does the shari^{c}a say about human rights ... about diplomatic immunities ... about the International Court of Justice ... about trade union rights ... about the use of nuclear weapons?

Finally, attention must be called to the fact that what the Western media find newsworthy about the Islamic resurgence tends to be items concerning the conservative-minded ^{c}ulama and their fundamentalism. This produces a misleading picture. By way of correction, it is necessary to emphasize that there are other intelligent Muslims who retain and practise their Islamic faith without insisting that they have nothing to learn from the West. These liberal-minded Muslims include statesmen and higher civil servants, writers and intellectuals, university professors in many fields, and others with a Western-type education. They are aware of what is good in the West, but not uncritically, for they have also seen something of the bad. They are committed to remaining faithful to Islam, but at the same time they realize that through his contacts with Western thought the intelligent Muslim of today has to seek answers to questions which are not asked in the traditional books. These intellectual needs of liberal-minded Muslims may help to explain two significant facts. In 1976 a Seerat Congress was held in Pakistan, attended by hundreds of Muslims, including two leading religious figures, the Imam of the Ka^{c}ba in Mecca, and the Shaikh of al-Azhar in Cairo, the leading traditional university. 'Seerat' is the life of Muhammad as exemplar, and the aim of the Congress was the spiritual uplift of Muslims - something like an Islamic eucharistic congress. What is worth noting in the present context is that the organizers saw fit to invite Christian scholars of Islam to deliver two of the seven plenary addresses. Again, in London in September 1981 at a meeting to inaugurate a new Islamic monthly called Arabia a large part of the main address by

Shaikh Yamani, the Arabian oil minister, was a call for more dialogue between Christians and Muslims. It is tempting to see in these facts an outcome of the realization by some Muslims that, if they are now wrestling with various intellectual problems, Christians have been wrestling with similar problems for a century or more and may conceivably be able to help them towards finding their own solutions.

REFERENCES

Daniel, N. (1960) Islam and the West, the Making of an Image, Edinburgh
Frye, R.N. (ed.) (1957) Islam and the West, 'S Gravenhage
Hitti, P.K. (ed.) (1962) Islam and the West, Princeton, N.J.
Rodinson, M. (1974) 'The Western Image and Western Studies of Islam' in Schacht J. and Bosworth C.E. (eds.) The Legacy of Islam, 2nd. ed., Oxford
Southern, R.W. (1962) Western Views of Islam in the Middle Ages, Cambridge, Mass.
Watt, W.M. (1972) The Influence of Islam on Medieval Europe, Edinburgh

ACCOUNTING FOR THE ORIENT

Bryan S. Turner

The way we talk about other people is a central problem of all human interaction and one of the constitutive debates within the social sciences. Although as a matter of fact we do talk about other people and other cultures apparently without too much difficulty, there are major philosophical problems which throw doubt on whether we can really understand people who belong to alien groups and foreign cultures. The philosophical issues are ones of translation and relativism. Sociologists and philosophers have come to see the meaning of words as dependent on their usage within a particular language, which in turn depends upon its setting within the way of life of a particular society. The philosophical task of understanding the meaning of an expression in another culture cannot, according to this view of language, be separated from the sociological problem of providing an exposition of the social structure within which that language is embedded(1). Taken as a strong doctrine about the dependence of meaning on social structure, such a philosophical position would render translation, if not impossible, at least uncertain and problematic. Unless there is extensive comparability of social structures, one language cannot be intelligibly translated into another. The paradox is that translation is a routine practice and becoming proficient in another language may be difficult but not impossible.

The question of translation can be treated as a specific instance of the more general problem of cultural relativism. The problem of relativism is as old as Western philosophy itself since it was Herodotus and Aristotle who confronted the fact that 'Fire burns both in Hellas and in Persia; but men's ideas of right and wrong vary from place to place'. If all beliefs and knowledge are culturally specific, then there are no universal criteria of truth, rationality and goodness by which social practices could be compared or evaluated. There are, however, a number of familiar difficulties with relativism, because, taken to its logical conclusion, it demonstrates that our knowledge of the world is merely ethnocentric, subjective preference. It would mean that no objective, valid comparisons between societies could be made and yet it would be difficult to conceive of knowledge which was not comparative or at least contained comparisons. To know something is, in principle, to be able to speak about it, and language necessarily involves contrasts and comparisons between sameness and difference. As with translation, we constantly compare, despite the apparently insoluble philosophical difficulties of doing so.

The questions of translation and relativism inevitably confront the sociologist who attempts a comparative study of two religions, such as Christianity and Islam. In fact, the question of adequate comparisons is so fundamental that it may appear to rule out such an enterprise from inception since the implication of much sociological analysis of Islam is that it is not a 'religion' at all, but a 'socio-political system'. The trouble with this implication is that it takes Christianity as a privileged model of what is to count as a 'religion' in the first place; perhaps in this respect it is Christianity, not Islam, which is the deviant case. One way into these conceptual puzzles may be to recognise that our contemporary views of other religions, such as Islam, are part of an established tradition of talking about alien cultlures. We understand other cultures by slotting them into a pre-existing code or discourse which renders their oddity intelligible. We are, in practice, able to overcome the philosophical difficulties of translation by drawing upon various forms of accounting which highlight differences in characteristics between 'us' and 'them'. The culture from which comparisons are to be made can be treated as possessing a number of essential characteristics - rationality, democracy, industrial progress - in terms of which other cultures are seen to be deficient. A table of positive and negative attributes is thus established by which alien cultures can be read off and summations arrived at. Any comparative study of religions will, therefore, tend to draw upon pre-existing assumptions and scholarly traditions which provide an interpretational matrix of contrasts and comparisons. The principal balance sheet by which Islam has been understood in Western culture may be referred to as 'Orientalism'.

Orientalism as a system of scholarship first emerged in the early fourteenth century with the establishment by the Church Council of Vienna of a number of university chairs to promote an understanding of Oriental languages and culture. The main driving force for Orientalism came from trade, inter-religious rivalries and military conflict. Knowledge of the Orient cannot, therefore, be separated from the history of European expansion into the Middle East and Asia(2). The discovery of the Cape route to Asia by Vasco de Gama in 1498 greatly extended the province of Orientalism, but it was not until the eighteenth and nineteenth centuries that detailed studies of Oriental societies were published in Europe. In Britain, the establishment of the Asiatic Society (of Bengal) in 1784 and the Royal Asiatic Society in 1823 were important landmarks in the development of Western attitudes. Similar developments took place in France with Napoleon's Institut d'Egypte and the Societe Asiatique in 1821, while in Germany an Oriental Society was formed in 1845. It was through these and similar institutions that knowledge of Oriental societies, studies of philology and competence in Oriental languages were developed and institutionalised. While in common sense terms the 'Orient' embraces an ill-defined geographical zone extending from the eastern shores of the Mediterranean to south-east Asia, Islam and the Islamic heart-lands played a peculiarly significant part in the formation of Western attitudes to the East.

Within the category of 'other religions', Islam has at least two major distinguishing features. First, Islam as a prophetic, monotheistic religion has very close ties historically and theologically with Christianity. It can be regarded, along with Christianity and Judaism, as a basic variant of the Abrahamic faith(3). Secondly, unlike other religions of the Orient, Islam was a major colonising force inside Europe and from the eight century onwards provided the dominant culture of southern Mediterranean societies. These two features of Islam raise the question: in what sense is Islam an 'Oriental religion'? This deceptively simple question in fact goes to the heart of the Orientalist problematic. If Orientalism addresses itself to the issue of what constitutes the Orient, then it is also forced ultimately to define the essence of Occidentalism. We might, for example, take a number of Christian cultural attributes - scriptural intellectualism, anti-magical rationality or the separation of the religious and the secular - as constitutive of Occidentalism in order to mark off the Orient. This strategy does immediately raise the difficulty that Christianity, as a Semitic, Abrahamic faith by origin, could be counted as 'Oriental', while Islam, as by expansion part of the culture of Spain, Sicily and eastern Europe, could be regarded as 'Occidental'. The problematic religious and geographical status of Islam was recognised by traditional Christian theology which either treated Islam as parasitic upon Judeo-Christian culture or as a schism within Christianity. In Dante's Divine Comedy, the Prophet Muhammad is constantly split in two as an eternal punishment for religious schism.

The problematic nature of Islam is not, however, merely a difficulty within Christian theology. If the motivating issue behind Christian Orientalism was the uniqueness of the Christian revelation with respect to Islamic heresy, then the crucial question for comparative sociology has been the dynamism of Western, industrial civilisation versus the alleged stagnation of the Orient. Within Weberian sociology, the fact that Islam is monotheistic, prophetic and ascetic raises important difficulties for the view that Protestant asceticism performed a critical role in the rise of Western rationality. In The Sociology of Religion(4), Weber provided two answers to remove this difficulty for the Protestant Ethic thesis. First, while recognising that Muhammad's initial message was one of ascetic self-control, Weber argued that the social carriers of Islam were Arab warriors who transformed the original salvation doctrine into a quest for land. Hence, the inner angst of Calvinism was never fully present in Islam. Secondly, the prebendal form of land-ownership in Islam resulted in a centralised state so that Islam became the ideology of a patrimonial structure and precluded the growth of urban asceticism(5). This argument about social carriers and patrimonial power in Islam permitted Weber to treat Islam as a religion of world acceptance with a formal and legalistic orientation to questions of personal salvation(6). Since Islam presented no radical challenge to the secular world of power, it failed to develop a rational theodicy which would, in principle, have driven believers to a significant position of world-mastery. Islam, by legitimating the status quo, never challenged the political structure in such a way to promote fundamental processes of social change.

Weber's treatment of Islam provides us with the accounting system that constitutes the basis of his comparative sociology of Oriental society, of which the central issue is a contrast between dynamic and stationary social systems. The task of Weber's sociology was to provide an historical account of the emergence of what he took to be the characteristic uniqueness of the West, namely the defining ingredients of rational capitalist production. These ingredients included rational (Roman) law, the modern state, the application of science to all areas of social life, especially to the technology of industrial production, the separation of the family from the business enterprise, autonomous urban institutions, an ascetic life-style which initially converted entrepreneurship into a 'calling' and finally the bureaucratisation of social procedures. These features of capitalist society were the institutional locations of a general process of rationalisation in which social relationships were increasingly subject to norms of calculation and prediction. The rationalisation of social life involved a continuous alienation of social actors, not only from the means of production, but from the means of mental production and from the military apparatus. The ownership of the means of economic, intellectual and military production are concentrated in bureaucratic, anonymous institutions so that, in Weber's view, capitalism became an 'iron cage' in which the individual is merely a 'cog'(7). While the individual is subjected to detailed social regulation, rational law, bureaucratic management and applied science provide the social conditions for economic stability by which capitalist accumulation can proceed unhindered by moral conventions or by capricious political intervention.

In Weber's sociology of Oriental society, an accounting system is created in which the Orient simply lacks the positive ingredients of Western rationality. Oriental society can be defined as a system of absences - absent cities, the missing middle class, missing autonomous urban institutions, the absence of legal rationality and the absence of private property(8). In Europe, Christianity permitted cities to arise in which urban social relations were based on a universal faith rather than on particular tribal loyalties; in addition, European cities enjoyed considerable economic and political independence from the state(9). In the Orient, according to Weber, cities did not evolve organically as economic centres, but were imposed on the countryside as military and political sites of state control. The Oriental city did not provide a congenial environment within which an urban bourgeoisie could emerge free from unpredictable, ad hoc political control. This analysis of the city in turn depends upon a basic contrast in Weber's sociology between the feudal structures of Europe and the prebendal organisation of land in the Orient. In feudalism where individual land-rights are inherited by a stable system of primogeniture or limited partibility, land-owning knights enjoy a degree of political freedom from feudal monarch in return for military service. In prebendalism, the prebend is a non-inheritable right which is controlled by a patrimonial state and therefore a stratum of cavalry is more directly subject to the royal household. While some forms of private land-ownership do occur in prebendalism, legal ownership of private land is restricted in scope and there is a strong tendency for the wealthy to avoid risk-taking capital investments. Hence, in Islam, Weber thought that capital was frequently frozen in the form of investment in religious property (waqf). While property was subject to political interference, it was also difficult to obtain legal security because religious law was essentially unstable. It is consequently possible to imagine Weber's comparative sociology as an accounting system with 'rational law', 'free cities', 'urban bourgeoisie' and the 'modern state' in one column and 'ad hoc law', 'military camps', 'state-controlled merchants' and 'patrimonial state' in the other. Weber does the work of translation from one set of social meanings to another context of meanings by a system of linguistic accounting in which Occidental categories have a privileged location.

It is often claimed that Weberian sociology represents a form of subjective idealism which unwittingly reproduces the contents of commonsense, bougeois thought and that, by contrast, the historical materialism of Karl Marx penetrates the conceptual surface of bourgeois political economy to reveal the objective structures which ultimately determine social life(10). This contrast is difficult to maintain in general terms and particular problems arise with the commentaries of Marx and Engels on Oriental society(11). In Marx and Engel's early journalist writing on India, China and the Middle East, we find the theoretical development of what has subsequently been referred to as 'the Asiatic mode of production'(12). The point of this theoretical device was to contrast the socio-economic stagnation of the Orient with the revolutionary character of capitalist society in which capitalists are forced to change constantly the technical basis of production in order to survive economically. The Asiatic mode of production is thus a form of social accounting which bears a close similarity to that employed by Weber. Marx and Engels, forming their theory on the basis of utilitarian analyses of India and Francois Bernier's Voyages (1710), focused their concern on the alleged absence of private property in land in Asia where the state controlled the distribution of land-ownership. In some of the journalistic work, such as his article on British rule in India(13), Marx emphasised the importance of climate and geography in the desert regions of North Africa and Asia in the rise of the state which had important functions in the control of irrigation works. Because the state controlled the land in order to manage public irrigation systems, social classes based on the ownership of property could not emerge and instead the population was held in a condition of what Engels called 'general (state) slavery'. In the absence of social classes and class struggle, there was no mechanism of social change. Since the history of all societies is the history of struggles between classes, it followed that Asia 'has no history at all, at least no known history'(14). In later works, such as Grundrisse and Capital, Marx shifted his attention away from the role of the state in irrigation to the nature of economic self-sufficiency of Asiatic villages as the ultimate explanation of Oriental stability. The outcome is still the same: the absence of radical changes in Asiatic social structure which, in Marx's terms, would count as historical change.

Weber and Marx adhered to rather similar accounting schemes to explain the presence of history in Occidental societies and its absence in the Orient. According to these schemes of translation, the Orient is a collection of gaps or a list of deficiencies – the absence of private property, the absence of social classes, the absence of historical changes in the mode of production. Since both Weber and Marx also adhered to the notion that state politics in the Orient were arbitrary and uncertain, their view of Oriental society may be regarded as yet another version of that more ancient system of accounting, namely 'Oriental despotism'. The theoretical impetus for the analysis of despotic politics came from the development of the absolutist state in Europe when philosophical discussions centred on the distinction between legitimate monarchy and arbitrary despotism. Thus, Benigne-Bossuet, instructor to Louis XIV, identified four principal causes of despotic rule which were the absence of private property, arbitrary laws, absolute political power and general slavery(15). These causes of despotism were all evident in the imperial structures of Russia and Turkey. A rather similar position was taken by Montesquieu in The Spirit of the Laws (1748) where he argued that despotism in the Asiatic empires was brought about by the absence of social institutions intervening between the absolute ruler and the general population who were consequently unprotected objects of the ruler's passions.

Whether or not Marx eventually abandoned the concept of the Asiatic mode of production has subsequently become an important issue in Marxist theory and politics(16). In recent years, a number of attempts have been made to jettison the concept by employing Louis Althusser's notion of an 'epistemological break' in the theoretical development of Marx's ideas. According to Althusser(17), it is possible to divide Marx's works into distinctive periods in which the early idealistic humanism of the Paris manuscripts was eventually replaced by an entirely new scientific interest in the objective laws of the capitalist mode of production. On these grounds it is possible to treat the concept of the Asiatic mode of production as a pre-scientific interest which Marx and Engels abandoned in their maturity. It has also been argued that, in any case, the concept is incompatible with the central element of the Marxist theory of the state as the product of a society divided along class lines. According to this view, class conflict is a 'condition of existence' of the state and, since in the Asiatic mode of production there are no classes, it is difficult to explain the existence of the state other than by vague references to 'climate and territory'(18). Unfortunately, these attempts to extricate Marx from an Orientalist problematic simply bring in their train a series of additional theoretical difficulties. Once the Asiatic mode of production has been abandoned, it is then necessary to conceptualise all pre-capitalist modes of production within the rather narrow framework of slavery or feudalism, unless Marxist theory is prepared to admit new additions to the existing orthodox list of modes of production.

The question which lies behind the accounting schemes of Marx and Weber concerns the social origins of capitalism in Western society and its absence in Oriental society. This question carries with it all the implications of the assumption about the uniqueness of the West, and therefore a dichotomous contrast between the progressive West and the stagnant East. There are two main theoretical strategies by which this basic question can be avoided. In the first, the question of capitalist origins in the Orient is inappropriate because the prior existence of European capitalism and the development of colonialism ruled out the autonomous development of capitalism outside Europe. European capitalism changed the global conditions for independent capitalism elsewhere by creating a world-wide system of economic dependency(19). The presence of capitalism in the Occident becomes the explanation for the absence of capitalism in the Orient. In the second strategy, it is possible to deny that capitalism has consistent social characteristics or uniform consequences. Just as England, France and Germany had unique developmental processes which cannot be subsumed under the general label of 'capitalist development', so each Oriental society is subject to individual, peculiar features which are contingent and historical. While both strategies are in some respects theoretically attractive, they are not without their own theoretical problems. The first solution is still left with the question: why then did capitalism emerge uniquely in the West? Any list of socio-economic causes to explain capitalism in the Occident implies the absence of such causes elsewhere. Furthermore, it is not entirely obvious that dependency theory or some notion of 'underdevelopment' will account for the absence of autonomous capitalist development outside Europe. The second solution would appear to rule out any law-like statements about the general characteristics of capitalism conceived as an abstract model of society in favour of empirical descriptions of particular developmental processes. The outcome of both positions might be the notion that capitalism is a purely contingent development. The alternative to Althusserian structuralism would be the position

> that industrialism was not written inevitably into the destiny of all agrarian society, but only emerged as a consequence of an accidental and almost improbable concatenation of circumstances which, it so happened, came together in the West.(20)

However, it is difficult to see how methodological accidentalism could be accepted as a general basis for a sociology of capitalism, which attempts to provide causal statements about the necessary connections between social structures, while also recognising that empirically these connections may be very complex and subject to contingent variations. The conclusion must be that Weberian sociology, on the one hand, and structuralist Marxism, on the other, have not developed entirely satisfactory responses to the accounting procedures of Orientalism.

As we have seen, much of the debate about pre-capitalist modes of production in English-speaking Marxism was initiated by a new interest in the French philosopher Louis Althusser. The reception of Althusserian Marxism was in the context of various attempts to provide a structuralist explanation of economic processes which did not involve restrictive economic reductionism and to provide a scientific alternative to the Hegelian idealism of the humanistic Marx. It was not until this debate was well established that it becaome clear that Althusser's emphasis on the proper "reading" of Marx's texts was part of a more general movement in French philosophy emerging out of literary criticism, semiology and discourse analysis. One of the crucial figures in the French context was Michel Foucault whose analysis of the relationship between power and knowledge subsequently became important in the critique of Orientalism. Foucault's ideas are notoriously difficult to summarise, but one important aspect of his general position is that any extension of systematic knowledge also involves an extension of power relations in society, which is manifested in more subtle and rigorous forms of social control over the body. Foucault's argument thus differs radically from a conventionally liberal perspective in which the evolution of knowledge out of ignorance requires a similar political evolution of freedom out of oppression. In the liberal view, the conditions for achieving knowledge through open debate involve fundamental political freedoms. For Foucault, the growth of penology, criminology, demography and other social sciences in the late eighteenth and nineteenth century corresponded to increasing political and social control over large masses of people within a confined urban space. More generally, these separate 'discourses' of the body constituted a dominant 'episteme' by which separate individuals could be categorised as different - as criminals, madmen, sexual perverts and so forth. All forms of language presuppose or create fundamental categories of sameness and difference and the application of these categories is an exercise of power by which one social group excludes another. The growth of systematic reasoning can be measured or indicated by the growth of time-tables, examinations, taxonomies and typologies which allocate individuals within a theoretical space just as Bentham's panopticon, the asylum, the class room and the hospital administer bodies within an organised social space. Historically speaking, the growth of scientific psychiatry corresponded with growth of asylum(21), the growth of penology with the prison(22), the development of clinical medicine with the hospital(23) and the discourse of sex with the confessional(24).

Within the perspective of Foucault's analysis of knowledge, we can now treat Orientalism as a discourse which creates typologies within which characters can be distributed: the energetic Occidental man versus the lascivious Oriental, the rational Westerner versus the unpredictable Oriental, the gentle white versus the cruel yellow man. The notion of Orientalism as a discourse of power emerging in the context of a geo-political struggle between Europe and the Middle East provides the basis for one of the most influential studies of recent times, namely Edward Said's Orientalism(25). Orientalism as a discourse divides the globe unambiguously into Occident and Orient; the latter is essentially strange, exotic and mysterious, but also sensual, irrational and potentially dangerous. This Oriental strangeness can only be grasped by the gifted specialist in Oriental cultures and in particular by those with skills in philology, language and literature. The task of Orientalism was to reduce the bewildering complexity of Oriental societies and Oriental culture to some manageable, comprehensible level. The expert, through the discourse on the Orient, represented the mysterious East in terms of basic frameworks and typologies. The Chrestomathy summarised the exotic Orient in a table of comprehensible items. The point of Orientalism, according to Said, was to orientalise the Orient and it did so in the context of fundamental colonial inequalities. Orientalism was based on the fact that we know or talk about the Orientals, while they neither know themselves adequately nor talk about us. There is no comparable discourse of Occidentalism. This is not to say that there have been no changes in the nature of Orientalism, but these changes tend to mask the underlying continuity of the discourse. The early philological and philosophical orientations of Sacy, Renan, Lane and Caussin have been replaced by an emphasis on sociology and economics in the new programme of 'area studies', but much of the underlying politics of power remains.

While Orientalism is an especially persistent discourse, Said believes that, given the changing balance of power in the modern world, there are signs of a new appreciation of the Orient and an awareness of the pit-falls of existing approaches. He thus pays tribute to such writers as Anwar Abdel Malek, Yves Lacoste and Jacques Berque and to the authors associated with the Review of Middle East Studies and the Middle East Research and Information Project (MERIP). These groups are both sensitive to the damaging legacy of Orientalism and to the need for new beginnings and different frameworks. Unfortunately, Said does not offer a detailed programme for the critique of Orientalism or for the creation of alternative perspectives. To some extent, he is content with a general rejection of ethnocentric frameworks:

> The more one is able to leave one's cultural home, the more one is able to judge it, and the whole world as well, with the spiritual detachment and generosity necessary for true vision. The more easily, too, does one assess oneself and alien cultures with the same combination of intimacy and distance.(26)

The problem of Said's attempted solution depends on how closely he wishes to follow Foucault's analysis of discourse.

The point of the critique of official psychiatry, established clinical medicine and contemporary discourses on sex is not, for Foucault, to present alternatives, since these would simply be themselves forms of discourse. In Foucault's perspective, there is no, as it were, discourse-free analysis. Given the nature of the modern world, we are constrained historically to:

the patient construction of discourses about discourses, and to the task of hearing what has already been said. (27)

For example, Foucault's analysis of medicine does not propose an alternative medicine or the absence of medicine; instead he attempts an archaeology of discourse, of the historical layers that are the conditions of discourse.

An adherence to Foucault's perspective on discourse as a critique of Orientalism might, therefore, result in somewhat negative and pessimistic conclusions. The contemporary analyses of Islam and the Middle East to which Said approvingly alludes turn out to be themselves discourses, corresponding to shifting power relationships between West and East. The Orientalist premise remains largely intact: I know the difference, therefore I control. There may, however, be one starting point which would be compatible with Said's universal humanism and Foucault's pessimism about discourse on discourses. It had been noted that language is organised in building-blocks of sameness and difference, but the main characteristic of Orientalism has been to concentrate on difference. In the case of Islam and Christianity, there is a strong warrant for looking at these aspects which unite rather than divide them, for concentrating on sameness rather than difference. We can then observe how common elements or themes are handled by Orientalist discourse as themes which are not 'really' the same or which in fact constitute departures and differences. As we have already commented, Islam and Christianity can be regarded as dimensions of a common, Semitic-Abrahamic religious stock. They have also been involved in processes of mutual colonisation, having common traditions of Jihad and Crusade. In this sense, it is possible to refer to Islam as an Occidental religion of Spain, Sicily, Malta, Yugoslavia and the Balkans and to Christianity as an Oriental religion of Syria, Egypt and North Africa. Islam and Christianity not only have important religious and geographical features in common, they also to a large extent share common frameworks in philosophy, science and medicine. Despite these overlapping cultural traditions, the general direction of Orientalism has always been to stress differences and separations. One particularly interesting illustration of this tendency is provided by the history of Western philosophy.

Islam and Christianity as religions of prophetic revelation were not initially equipped to provide a philosophical framework within which to present and discuss the theological problems of orthodoxy. Furthermore, they were both early on confronted by a powerful tradition of secular logic and rhetoric which was the legacy of Greece. The Aristotelianism which became the major Christian framework for the philosophical formulation of Christian beliefs was transmitted by Islamic scholars - Averroes, Avicenna, al-Kindi and al-Razi. Here, therefore, is an area of common experience and historical development, where mediaeval Christian culture was dependent on Islam. The Orientalist response to this historical connection has been to argue that Islam was merely a medium between Hellenism and the Occident. Islamic scholarship neither contributed to nor improved upon the Greek heritage which eventually found its 'true' home in fifteenth and sixteenth century European science and technology. The notion of an Islamic contribution to Western culture was attacked, for example, in the nineteenth century by the French Orientalist and philosopher Ernest Renan. He argued that Islamic civilisation was incompatible with scientific advance:

> All those who have been in the East, or in Africa, are
> struck by the way in which the mind of the true
> believer is fatally limited by the species of iron circle
> that surrounds the head, rendering it absolutely closed
> to knowledge, incapable of either learning anything, or
> being open to any new idea. (28)

By extension, Renan suggested that science in Islam could and did only flourish when the prescriptions of orthodox theology were relaxed. One illustration of this position was Renan's sympathetic response to the Muslim reformer Jamal al-Din al-Afghani, whose overt orthodoxy was matched by a covert, elitist rationalism. Finally, Renan claimed that the great majority of so-called Arab scientists and philosophers were in fact 'Persians, Transoxians, Spaniards, natives of Bokhara, of Samarcand, of Cordova, of Seville'.

This view of Islam as merely the sterile transmitter of Greek philosophy and science to European civilisation has subsequently been re-affirmed, although often with more subtlety and less prejudice. Bertrand Russel dismissively commented in his history of Western philosophy that Arabic philosophy was not significant as original thought. A similar line of argument was taken by O'Leary in How Greek Science Passed to the Arabs(29), where it was argued that Islamic philosophers were mainly important as translators of Greek culture. Although he recognised the importance of Muslim scientists in such fields as medicine, optics and chemistry, he treated Islamic thought as the property of a 'privileged coterie'. The great attraction of seeing our philosophical, cultural and scientific inheritance as based upon Greek culture and of seeing Islam as simply a neutral vehicle for the transmission of those values is that it allows us to connect scientific freedom of thought with political democracy. The major contribution of Greek society to Western thought was logical and rhetorical modes of argumentation, permitting the systematisation of debate and inquiry. These modes of analysis arose because of the need in the Greek polity for open, public dialogue. Once more it is possible thereby to contrast the Oriental despotic tradition of closed, centralised authority with the Greek model of democracy requiring open, uninhibited discourse. The association of freedom and truth has thus become a central theme of Western philosophers occupying very different positions within the political spectrum. While in other respects in profound disagreement, there is an ironic agreement between Karl Popper and Jurgen Habermas that knowledge requires an open society. The problem with this emphasis on Hellenism and democratic inquiry is that it ignores the fact that Greek society was based on slavery and that the majority of the population was, therefore, precluded from these open debates between citizens.

The debate about the ultimate origins of Occidentalism and the connections between Islam and Christianity via Greek philosophy raises the question of whether the dynamism of Western culture lies within a Christian legacy or in Hellenism. To illustrate the point of this observation it is enough to recall that against writers like Werner Sombart in The Jews and Modern Capitalism, Weber sought the origins of the ethos of modern society in Protestant asceticism, whereas Marx traced the secular/critical content of Western thought back to Heraclitus. In general, those writers who are indifferent or critical towards Christianity are likely to underline the Greek roots of Western society; in addition, they often take a sympathetic view of Islam as the basis for their criticisms of it. This position is characteristic of, for example, Friedrich Nietzsche. Thus, while Orientalism has so far been treated as a form of negative accounting stressing the absences within Islamic society, it is also possible to detect forms of positive accounting which adopt certain features of Islam as the means of a rational critique of Christianity. The contents of Oriental society may thus not be the central issue for Orientalism, but rather it raises the questions about the constitutive features of Occidental society. While what we may call theistic Orientalism adopted Christian values as the counter-weight to Islam as a deviant religion, agnostic Orientalism treated Greek culture as the true source of Western values, often incidentally treating Islam as a more rational form of monotheism than Christianity.

It is possible to indicate the complexity of these relationships between Occidentalism, Orientalism and Hellenism in Western philosophy by a brief comparison of Hume and Nietzsche. While there has been much disagreement over the nature of Hume's philosophy of religion(30), it will be sufficient for this present argument to concentrate on his celebrated contrast of the virtues of polytheism and monotheism. In the Natural History of Religion, Hume argued that polytheism is the ancient religion of all primitive people and that monotheism developed later with the advance of rationalism, especially in the argument from design. While there is this historical development from polytheism, there is also a constant swing backwards and forwards between these two types of theistic belief, since the vulgar and ignorant tend, in any society, towards polytheism. On the whole, the advantages to mankind of polytheism are greater than those arising from monotheism. The latter is associated with intolerance, exaggerated asceticism and abasement. When the gods are only marginally superior to mortal men, a more open, friendly and egalitarian attitude towards them is possible:

> Hence activity, spirit, courage, magnanimity, love of liberty , and all the virtues which aggrandize a people.(31)

The principal advantage of monotheism is that it is more 'comformable to sound reason', but this very fact brings about an alliance between theology and philosophy which in turn leads to a stultifying scholasticism. Since Hume holds that Islam is a stricter form of theism than is Christianity with its trinitarian doctrine, it follows that Islam is 'conformable to sound reason', but this also means that Hume regarded Islam as an intolerant, narrow religion. In regard to rationality, therefore, Islam is favourably contrasted with Christianity and, furthermore, Hume humorously refers to Islam as a means of illustrating the absurdity of Roman Catholic doctrines of the Eucharist. A Turkish prisoner was once brought to Paris by his Russian captor and some doctors of the Sorbonne decided to convert this captive to Christianity. Having been catechised and taken first communion, the Muslim prisoner was asked how many gods there were and replied that there were no gods, since he had just eaten Him! The point of this Hume illustration is to show that, while Said largely treats Orientalism as a negative accounting system, in the hands of a rationalist philosopher, Islam can be used as a positive critique of the 'absurdity' of Christian doctrines.

This critical attitude towards Christianity was especially prominent in Nietzsche's philosophy. In The Genealogy of Morals, Nietzsche claimed that Christian morality had its social origins in the resentment of the Jews against their oppressors; the doctrine of turning the other cheek and altruistic love are in fact moral doctrines of a slave class giving vent to feelings of inferiority and suppression. Christian morality has its location in the psychological revolt of slaves against masters:

> It was the Jews who, in opposition to the aristocratic equation (good = beautiful = happy = loved by the gods), dared with a terrifying logic to suggest the contrary equation, and indeed to maintain in the teeth of the most profound hatred (the hatred of weakness) this contrary equation, namely 'the wretched are alone the good; the poor, the weak, the lowly, are alone the good.(32)

Nietzsche regarded the critical spirit of Socrates as the supreme root of true virtues of self-development, criticism and heroic independence. While Nietzsche compared favourably the self-sacrifice of Socrates and Jesus for an ideal, he regarded Christianity as a system of conventional morality which destroyed individual creativity and critical thought(33). It was from this perspective that Nietzsche came to see the slave morality of Christianity as the negation of the heroic virtues of Socrates and Muhammad. In the Anti-Chrst, Nietzsche declared that:

> Christianity robbed us of the harvest of the culture of the ancient world, it later went on to rob us of the harvest of the culture of Islam. The wonderful Moorish cultural world of Spain, more closely related to us at bottom, speaking more directly to our senses and taste, than Greece and Rome, was trampled down...why? because it was noble, because it owed its origins to manly instincts, because it said Yes to life even in the rare and exquisite treasures of Moorish life!(34)

Nietzsche's positive evaluation of Islam in general and of Islamic Spain in particular cannot be readily understood in terms of Said's view of Orientalism, but they are comprehensible within a scheme of positive, secularist Orientalism which employs Islam as the basis for a critique of Christianity.

The problems of translation and comparison which lie at the heart of sociology and religious studies have been implicitly resolved by the creation of accounting schemes which establish hierarchies of sameness and difference. In the study of Islam and Asiatic society, the dominant accounting procedure is Orientalism which seeks to explain the nature of Islamic culture by negation so that Islamdom is constituted by its absences. In recent years the Orientalist tradition has

23

been heavily criticised, but no radical alternative has yet emerged and, in terms of a pessimistic perspective on the nature of discourse, it is difficult to see how any valid alternative could emerge. The critique of Orientalism has largely neglected two possible routes out of the conventional discourse on the Orient. Alongside negative accounting schemes, there has also been a positive view of Oriental rationality on the part of secular philosophers who have employed Islam as a mirror to indicate the absurdity of Christian faith, but in this option is merely accounting in reverse. Following Foucault's analysis of the archaeology of knowledge, Said has studied the various ways in which a persistent Orientalism has been founded on a contrast of differences, but a language of the Orient would also generate, in principle, an account of sameness. One solution to theological ethnocentrism, on these grounds, would be to emphasise those points of contact and sameness which unite the Christian, Jewish and Islamic traditions into merely variations on a religious theme which in unison provide the bases of our culture.

NOTES

1. Winch, P., The Idea of a Social Science (London, 1958)
2. Kiernan, V.G., The Lords of Human Kind (Harmondsworth, 1972)
3. Hodgson, M.G.S., The Venture of Islam, 3 vols. (Chicago, 1974)
4. London, 1966
5. Turner, B.S. 'Orientalism, Islam and Capitalism', Social Compass, 25 (1978), pp. 371-394.
6. Freund, J., The Sociology of Max Weber (London, 1968)
7. Weber, M., The Sociology of Religion (London 1966); Loewith, K., 'Max Weber and Karl Marx', in Wrong D. (ed.) Max Weber (Englewood Cliffs, N.J., 1970) pp. 101-121.
8. Turner, B.S., Marx and the End of Orientalism (London, 1978)
9. Weber, M., The City (New York, 1958)
10. Hirst, P.Q., Social Evolution and Sociological Categories (London, 1976)
11. Turner, B.S., For Weber, essays in the sociology of fate (London, 1981)
12. Avineri, S. (ed.) Karl Marx on Colonialism and Modernization (New York, 1968)
13. Marx, K., 'The future results of the British rule in India' (1853) in Marx, K. and Engels, F., On Colonialism (New York, 1972)
14. Ibid., p. 81.

15. Stelling-Michaud, S., 'Le mythe du despotisme oriental', Schweizer Beitrage zur Allgemeinen Geschichte, 18, (1960), pp. 328-346.
16. Wittfogel, K., Oriental Despotism, a comparative study of total power (New Haven and London, 1957)
17. Althusser, L. For Marx (Harmondsworth, 1969)
18. Hindess, B. and Hirst, P.Q., Pre-Capitalist Modes of Production (London, 1975)
19. Frank, A.G., Sociology of Underdevelopment and the Underdevelopment of Sociology (London, 1972)
20. Gellner, E., 'In defence of Orientalism', Sociology, 14 (1980), p. 296.
21. Foucault, M., Madness and Civilisation (London, 1967)
22. Idem., Discipline and Punish (London, 1977)
23. Idem., The Birth of the Clinic (London, 1973)
24. Idem., The History of Sexuality (London, 1979)
25. Said, E.W., Orientalism (London, 1978)
26. Ibid., p. 259.
27. Foucoult, Birth of the Clinic, p. xvi.
28. Renan, E., 'Islamism and Science' in The Poetry of the Celtic Races and Other Studies (London, 1896), p. 85.
29. O'Leary, de Lacy, How Greek Science Passed to the Arabs (London, 1969)
30. Gaskin, J.C.A., 'Hume's critique of religion', Journal for the History of Philosophy, 14 (1976) pp. 301-311; Capaldi, N., David Hume, the Newtonian philosopher (Boston, 1975); Williams, B.A.O., 'Hume on Religion' in Pears, D.F., (ed.), Hume: a symposium (London, 1963), pp. 77-88.
31. Hume, D. On Religion (London), 1963) p. 68.
32. Nietzsche, F., The Genealogy of Morals, a polemic (Edinburgh, 1910) p. 30.
33. Kaufmann, W., Nietzsche, philosopher, psychologist, antichrist (Princeton, N.J., 1950).
34. Nietzsche, F., The Anti-Christ (Harmondsworth, 1968) p. 183.

REFERENCES

Althusser, L. (1969) For Marx, Harmondsworth
Avineri, S. (ed.) (1968) Karl Marx on Colonialism and Modernization, New York
Capaldi, N. (1975) David Hume, the Newtonian philosopher, Boston
Foucault, M. (1967) Madness and Civilisation, London
Idem., (1973) The Birth of the Clinic, London
Idem., (1977) Discipline and Punish, London
Idem., (1979) The History of Sexuality, London
Freund, J. (1968) The Sociology of Max Weber, London
Frank, A.G. (1972) Sociology of Underdevelopment and the Underdevelopment of Sociology, London

Gaskin, J.C.A. (1976) 'Hume's critique of religion', Journal for the History of Philosophy, 14, pp. 301-11

Gellner, E. (1980) 'In defence of Orientalism', Sociology, 14, pp. 295-300

Hindess, B. and Hirst P.Q. (1975) Pre-Capitalist Modes of Production, London

Hirst, P.Q. (1976) Social Evolution and Sociological Categories, London

Hodgson, M.G.S. (1974) The Venture of Islam, 3 Vols., Chicago

Hume, D. (1963) On Religion, London

Kaufmann, W. (1950) Nietzsche, philosopher, psychologist, antichrist, Princeton, New Jersey

Kiernan, V.G. (1972) The Lords of Human Kind, Harmondsworth

Koebner, R. (1951) 'Despot and despotism, vicissitudes of a political term', Journal of the Warburg and Courtauld Institutes, 14, pp. 275-302

Loewith, K. (1970) 'Max Weber and Karl Marx' in Dennis Wrong (ed.) Max Weber, Englewood Cliffs, N.J.

Marx, K. (1972) 'The future results of the British rule in India' (1853) in Karl Marx and F. Engels On Colonialism, New York

Nietzsche, F. (1910) The Genealogy of Morals, a polemic, Edinburgh

Idem., (1968) The Anti-Christ, Harmondsworth

O'Leary, de Lacy (1969) How Greek Science Passed to the Arabs, London

Renan, E. (1896) 'Islamism and science' in The Poetry of the Celtic Races and Other Studies, London

Said, E.W. (1978) Orientalism, London

Stelling-Michaud, S. (1960) 'Le mythe du despotisme oriental' Schweizer Beitrage zur Allgemeinen Geschichte, 18-19, pp. 328-46

Turner, B.S. (1978) 'Orientalism, Islam and capitalism' Social Compass, 25, pp. 371-94

Idem., (1978) Marx and the End of Orientalism, London

Idem., (1981) For Weber, essays in the sociology of fate, London

Weber, M. (1958) The City, New York

Idem., (1966) The Sociology of Religion, London

Idem., (1966) The Protestant Ethic and the Spirit of Capitalism, London

Williams, B.A.O. (1963) 'Hume on religion', in D.F. Pears (ed.) Hume: a symposium, London

Winch, P. (1958) The Idea of a Social Science, London

Wittfogel, K. (1957) Oriental Despotism, a comparative study of total power, New Haven and London

ISLAM AND JUDAISM

John F.A. Sawyer

Outside of comparative religion syllabuses and departments of Religious Studies, Islam and Judaism do not very often appear together. The reasons for this are not hard to find. Islam is the official religion of most of the Arab countries, while Judaism is the official religion of Israel. Jews, including a large proportion of Israelis (although not now the majority), are westernized, possessing close social and cultural links with Europe and the United States. The overwhelming majority of Muslims, however, live in Africa, Asia and the Middle East, and are distinct, socially and culturally, from the West. Furthermore, experts in Arabic and Islamic Studies do not often possess expertise in Hebrew and Judaic Studies and vice versa, and to a casual observer the two religions, in spite of their common roots, would appear to have very few similarities. The language and literature of Judaism could hardly be more different from the languages and literatures of Islam, the synagogue from the mosque, the Jew from the Muslim.

The relationship is nonetheless an intriguing and important one, not only from a purely historical point of view, but also - and this is why it has been included in the present collection - because, as is well known, religious factors have always played a part in Middle Eastern politics and probably always will. Any effort, therefore, to promote understanding and mutual respect between Muslim and Jew will inevitably have a bearing on Arab-Israeli relations as well. I shall therefore look first at some historical questions concerning, in particular the Qur'an and Muhammad's relations with the Jews of his day, then at relations between Jews and Muslims in the Middle Ages, and, finally, at the situation today.

There are many references to the Jews in the Qur'an and most of them are hostile. Certainly they are described as a people chosen 'above all beings'(Qur'an 44:32), and included among 'the People of the Book' (e.g. 59:2), together with believers and Christians upon whom 'no fear shall come neither shall they sorrow' (2:62; 5:69). God blessed the Children of Israel and preferred them above all beings (2:44, 116; 45:15), but because of their disobedience and obstinacy, He rejected them, and that is the situation in most of the passages in which they are mentioned. They are 'those on whom God's anger rests' (58:15), 'the most hostile of men towards believers' (5:82), and the latter are instructed not to make friends with them (5:56). Some of the Biblical stories seem to have been selected deliberately to present the Jews in a bad light: Sura 2 (al-baqara) the longest chapter of the Qur'an, for example, tells how they worshipped the Golden Calf, transgressed the sabbath, broke the covenant, rejected the prophets and so on. The same Sura mentions the doctrine of tahrif, (2:75) according to which the Jews (like the Christians) 'tampered' with the sacred scriptures so that the Hebrew text of the Bible is corrupt and unreliable or, according to another form of the doctrine, their interpretation of the sacred text is corrupt and unreliable. In a really pointed simile, the Jews entrusted with the Law of Moses are likened to an ass carrying a load of books on its back (62:5).

And there is another kind of anti-Jewish teaching in the Qur'an: the deliberate avoidance of Jewish customs. There are some glaring examples in the second Sura: in an explicitly anti-Jewish gesture, the Prophet calls upon his followers at Medina to face Mecca, not Jerusalem, when they pray: to turn their backs, in other words, on Jerusalem. (2:143-4) According to the Qur'an, Abraham and his son actually built the Ka'ba at Mecca (2:127). When Muhammad made Mecca the focus for prayers, not Jerusalem, the effect was to turn Islam away from the latter city, away from the Holy Land and away from Judaism. The importance of Jerusalem as a Muslim shrine today goes back to a connection with the Prophet's apocalyptic vision known as the 'Night Journey' (al-mi'raj; 17:1). This connection was stressed by the Umayyad Caliphs, one of whom built the exquisite Dome of the Rock on the site, and by modern Muslims, influenced no doubt by the events of 1948 and 1967 as much as by anything, but it has never had the same central religious significance for Muslims as it has for Jews. Other deliberate moves to dissociate Islam from Judaism might include the choice of Friday as the day for congregational worship instead of Saturday; (62:9) five prayer times each day instead of three; the month long fast of Ramadan 'wherein the Qur'an was sent down to be a guidance to the people' (2:185), in place of the one-day fast of Yom Kippur. There are still traces of this fast in the Qur'an (2:183), and it is interesting to note in passing that in Shi'i Islam the high point of the calendar is the fast of 'Ashura on the tenth day of Muharram, when the martyrdom of Husain at Karbala is commemorated. Ramadan, however, is the major fast in the Qur'an, obligatory on all Muslims, and again replaces the Jewish fast. In many instances it seems as though these were deliberate changes of policy on the part of the Prophet, turning his followers away from the Jews and decisively separating Islam from Judaism. There are historical reasons for these developments during the life of the Prophet (asbab al-nuzul or 'occasion of revelation' as they are called by Muslim scholars). Mecca, where Muhammad grew up, was a cosmopolitan city. Muhammad must certainly have been familiar with many biblical and other Judaeo-Christian traditions, and there has been some debate in modern times on the question of his sources. Some have argued these were primarily Jewish: familiar biblical stories often contain legendary material that corresponds very closely to post-Biblical traditions. For example, the elaborate version of the legend of Solomon and the Queen of Sheba sounds as though it has come straight out of the Jewish Targum: in both the hoopoe was the bird that brought Solomon news of the fabulous Queen, and in both he makes her walk on a glass floor so that he can have a closer look at her legs (27:16-44). The same applies to the Qur'anic variation of the Joseph story (Sura 11) and many others. Did Muhammad have at some time close and fruitful contacts with Jewish rabbis? There now seem to be several convincing reasons why this is unlikely to be the case,

Firstly, contacts with Christians at Mecca are a priori far more likely. Christian missionaries were a familiar sight in 6th and 7th century Mecca, and their preaching in the market-place gave a currency to Christian traditions that the far more closed world of Jewish rabbinic exegesis never had. In fact, in lists of Muhammad's earliest followers Christians do occur, but no Jews. Secondly, the legendary variations on Biblical themes are just as common in the Syrian and Ethiopic literature of Eastern Christianity as they are in Jewish literature. It is often hard to tell which came first: the Christian, the Jewish or the Muslim. Besides, New Testament traditions and legendary additions to New Testament stories (like the legend of Jesus making a clay bird and breathing life into it) appear just as frequently in the Qur'an as Old Testament traditions, and there is no question about their source. Finally the anti-Jewish slant that we have noted in the Qu'ranic version of many Biblical stories is, one has to admit, only too common in the exegetical traditions of much early Christian literature as well. This means that some of the anti-Jewish polemic in Sura Two and elsewhere could go back to a time before Muhammad came into contact with the Jews, and does not necessarily presuppose any contacts between him and the Jews of his day.

On the other hand, when we come to look at the Medinan period and Muhammad's treatment of the Jews there, it must be said that many of the anti-Jewish attitudes in the Qur'an do fit into his early years as leader of the Muslim community there. The situation at Medina when he arrived in 622 was

29

complicated in the extreme: that there were Jews there in positions of authority and influence is certain; but many Jews were indistinguishable from their Arab neighbours. Families had been there for many years and had assumed Arab names. There must have been intermarriage and some Arabs may have adopted the Jewish religion. In some sources quite a number of Arab clans are actually designated Jewish.

Another complication is that many of our sources may have been written at a time when relations between the Jews and their Muslim rulers were strained: at about the time when Ibn Ishaq (d.circa 761 A.D.) was writing his extremely influential Life of the Prophet, for example, there had been at least one Jewish messianic revolt in which Issa ibn Obadyahu led 10,000 Jews against the Umayyad Caliph al-Mansur. He and other writers may have allowed contemporary attitudes and perspectives to interfere with objective history-writing, a problem of our own time too, to which we shall be returning later.

At any rate, all our sources (excepting the Qur'an itself, which almost never names names) give the names of three Jewish clans, powerful factors in the complex political and economic scene that confronted Muhammad when he arrived in Medina in 622: al-Nadir and Qurayza were wealthy land owners possessing some of the richest agricultural assets in the oasis; and Qaynuqa^c were skilled craftsmen, mainly goldsmiths, who controlled an important corner of the market in that region.

Most sources are agreed that the Banu Qaynuqa^c were besieged and expelled from Medina by the Prophet in 624; al-Nadir was expelled in 625, and in 627 the adult males of the clan Qurayza were put to death to a man on the Prophet's orders. It would be very odd if these events did not leave their mark on the Medinan Suras of the Qur'an.

The first thing to note is that these were not, in fact, the only tribes to have been treated by the prophet in this way. It would be wrong to deduce that the Qur'an reflects any kind of systematic plan to expel all Jews from the Islamic state in Medina. In fact the so called constitution of that state includes many references to the Jews as though a natural part of the new community. His attacks on these three Jewish tribes were probably motivated primarily by the same strategic considerations as those which motivated his other campaigns. They were a threat to the unity and stability of the young community. There were numerous isolated cases of treachery on both sides that provided the immediate causes. Their wealth and influence must have been greatly coveted too. But all these factors do not add up to peculiarly anti-Jewish hostility.

It does seem likely that at first Muhammad hoped to gain the support of the three tribes by peaceful means and this may have meant adopting Jewish customs. We have already mentioned his initial designation of Jerusalem as the qibla (focus of prayers), and Yom Kippur may be another example. But when he failed to win them over, he turned against them both in his religious teachings and by force of arms; turning away from Jerusalem to face Mecca, putting a new emphasis on Abraham as a model rather than Moses (who was too Jewish), and then attacking and destroying or expelling those three tribes - though probably not all the other Jews.

It seems that both the anti-Jewish polemic of Meccan Christians and the clash between Muhammad and the Jews at Medina have left their mark on the Qur'an: neither the Meccan nor the Medinan Suras have much to say in favour of the Jews or Judaism. The earliest phase was a phase when at all levels it seems that Islam and Judaism were poles apart and for anyone interested in the two religions, there is hardly any kind of positive influence one way or the other.

The second period to be discussed is characterised by the closest co-operation between Jews and Muslims - the Golden Age of what has been called Hebraeo-Arabic thought. This was the age that produced such intellectual giants as the philosopher and physician Avicenna and Maimonides, best known and most influential of all mediaeval Jewish philosophers, who became physician to Saladin, viceroy of Egypt, to name but two of the greatest.

So closely intertwined were the Islamic and Jewish cultures in those halcyon days that it is often hard to know whether a work is of Jewish origin or not. For example, it was not until the 19th century that Avicebron, another of the leading philosophers of the period, was identified with the 11th century Jewish scholar Solomon ibn Gabirol. The Arabic writer Averroes of Cordoba, considered by some to have been an early evolutionist, had more influence upon Jewish thinkers than on Muslims or Christians. Perhaps the best symbol of this remarkable age of enlightenment in the history of Muslim-Jewish relations is the exquisite synagogue at Toledo, completed in 1357. Hence the Hebrew and Arabic inscriptions form so essential a part of the design that they survive to this day despite the fact that it was later converted into a Christian Church.

In this connection it is worth remembering that the year 1492 was not only the year in which Christopher Columbus discovered America: it was also the year of the expulsion of the Jews from Spain. Ten years after Muslim Spain had been conquered by Christendom, something like 160,000 Jews were expelled from Spain and took refuge under Muslim rulers in North Africa, Egypt and Palestine, where Jewish and Islamic scholarship continued to flourish for several centuries. Safed in northern Israel is a good example: at the beginning of the 16th century it became the capital, so to speak, of Jewish mysticism, producing saints and scholars like Joseph Caro and Isaac Luria.

Of course, a survey, however cursory, of Jews under Islam in the Middle Ages would have to allude to occasional Jewish rebellions against the Muslim authorities, like that of Issa ibn Obadyahu already mentioned; the conversions of Jews, like the celebrated 17th century charismatic Shabbetai Zvi, to Islam; and acts of Muslim oppression such as the imprisonment and ransom of the Jewish citizens of Safed by the Ottoman ᶜAbd Allah Pasha in 1819. But on the whole, from the beginning of the ᶜAbbasid period when Baghdad became capital of the Islamic empire, until the present century, the history of Muslim-Jewish relations is one of, at worst, peaceful co-existence, at best highly productive cross-fertilization at all levels.

Not quite at all levels, for that of religious beliefs and practices cannot be included. For every example of philosophical, scientific or political co-operation between Jews and Muslims, one could cite several examples of religious isolationism or conservatism. Let me quote one: Judah ha-Levi, Jewish philosopher and one of mediaeval Spain's greatest poets, who was born in Toledo about 1085, was much influenced in his philosophy by the mighty Muslim philosopher and mystic al-Ghazali and in his poetry by Arabic metre and style. But in his best known prose work, Al-Cuzari, he argues for the superiority and independence of his own religion with a single mindedness that verges on crudity. Al-Cuzari is a pagan king who invites three philosophers, a Christian, a Muslim and a Jew, to his court to describe their respective beliefs. Needless to say the Jew wins the debate, such as it is, the others being depicted as unsubtle and unattractive. The Jew also, incidentally, (in spite of Judah ha-Levi's own superb Arabic-style compositions) argues that the use of foreign metres destroys the essence of the Hebrew language: It is interesting how common this ambivalent attitude is, on both sides: while they co-operated throughout the period so productively (often united against the common Christian oppressor), the religions remained strictly apart. There was ignorance and prejudice on both sides, and virtually no communication.

Finally we come to the relation between Islam and Judaism today. What effect has the emergence of the State of Israel had on Muslim-Jewish relations? What new light has been shed, if any, on the Qur'an and the origins of Islam by modern scholarship? Have conditions for dialogue between Jews and Muslims changed today?

In the first place, both Islamic Studies and Jewish Studies over the last 100 years have inevitably been influenced by historical events. The 19th century Jewish historian Heinrich Graetz, for example, all too familiar with the pogroms and deportations of Jews in Tsarist Russia in his own day, and with the rise of intellectual anti-Semitism in 19th century Europe, contrasted the easy life of the Jews under Muslim rule with their miserable persecuted existence under the Christians. He was probably right, but Leon Nemoy, another Jewish historian, writing on the same subject in 1956, on the eve of the Israeli occupation of Sinai, accuses Graetz of pro-Muslim bias. Another example of how scholarship and politics can get enmeshed with one another is the highly controversial work of Patricia Crone and Michael Cook entitled Hagarism: The Making of the Islamic World. Using contemporary non-Muslim sources, mainly Syriac-Christian and Jewish texts the authors argue that Islam was originally a variety of Jewish messianism, (they call it Hagarism), and that later Islam was a decline from that early pinnacle, to 'Sadducee Islam'. It amounts to a very radical rewriting of Islamic history, but, more than that, a rewriting that presents orthodox Islam in a most unfavourable light. This is not the place to attempt a detailed critique of this, in parts, implausible theory, but let me say two things about it. Firstly there have been very few studies of the subject which take account of all the sources, simply because so few people can handle the sources in Arabic as well as Syriac, Hebrew and Ethiopic. Crone and Cook, together with a few other scholars in the Oriental Institute, Oxford, and the School of Oriental and African Studies, London, have made a start. Secondly, the authors can hardly have been so ingenuous as to have overlooked the possible effects of their work in the present climate. In fact researchers can hardly help taking sides, and although this kind of motivation may on occasion produce new theories that will stand the test of time, one cannot but deplore the academic damage that such a situation can cause.

One more example of the effect of recent political history upon history writing is less depressing. It is an interesting monograph on Muhammad and the Jews by India's High Commissioner to Trinidad and Tobago, Dr Barakat Ahmad. Anxious at every stage of his argument to make allowances for the bias of his sources, he rejects as legendary both the mass execution of the Banu Qurayza and the expulsion of the Banu Qaynuqa^c. Again, his purpose may not be primarily ecumenical or conciliatory, but as the former adviser to the Indian Delegation to the United Nations Central Assembly, he cannot have been unaware of what he was doing when he published this historical research in 1979.

So much for some recent historians in their historical context. What about the study of the two religions in the modern climate? So far we have noted only differences: having said that both religions are monotheistic, that is about as far as one can go. Both trace their spiritual ancestry back to Abraham, but, as we saw, the Muslim Abraham who, with his son Ishmael, built the Ka^{c}ba at Mecca, is very different from the Jewish Abraham, to whom God promised to give a land stretching from Egypt to Syria and who with his son

Isaac, sacrificed a ram on the Temple Mount at Jerusalem. Both honour the prophets, but Muslims give peculiar honour to Jesus and Muhammad, while for Jews, Jesus is at best just another rabbi, and Muhammad an Arabian visionary. The fact is these two religions developed independently for centuries and now have virtually nothing in common. Far from attempting to discover common ground, dialogue in this case means removing ignorance and prejudice on both sides. Some kind of dialogue does go on in various places: there is, for example, a European Jewish-Christian-Muslim Council with a branch in London. The so-called Rainbow Group incorporating members of a wide spectrum (Muslim, Christian and Jewish) began in Jerusalem about 15 years ago and it too has a branch in London now.

According to some commentators such as Alister Cooke, the Camp David talks were made easier by the religious beliefs of the three leaders, an orthodox Jew, a devout Muslim and a conservative Christian from Plains, Georgia. It does seem likely that other less mystical and more tangible factors predominated at Camp David. Nevertheless it is hard enough to discover instances of serious dialogue between Muslims and Jews such that each side learns to respect each other.

At the risk of appearing superficial or presumptuous or both, I would like to end by offering two observations which seem to me to be important in this connection. First, both Jews and Christians tend to look on Islam as a younger religion, derivative and therefore less valid. I believe this to be based on a misconception. Judaism, Christianity and Islam cannot be simply placed in such a crude chronological sequence. The fact is Judaism does not exist without the Talmudic sources of 4th and 5th centuries A.D., not to mention the mediaeval commentaries; nor does Christianity exist without the patristic sources, not to mention mediaeval and modern developments. In that time scale Islam is not younger, or more derivative than either Judaism or Christianity. In any case while the antiquity argument may convince Jews or Christians of their superiority, it carries no weight with Muslims since they see their religion as the final revelation, their Prophet as the 'seal of the prophets'. Oldest is not necessarily best, and I hope I have shown how independent Islam and Judaism are, and how important it is to keep questions of ancient history and sources in their proper perspective.

This brings me to the other point I want to conclude with: the diversity of Judaism and the diversity of Islam. Today, neither religion is monolithic, and no discussion of relations between Jews and Muslims would be complete without mentioning this fact. New forms of Islam and new forms of Judaism have emerged and with them new attitudes among men and women disillusioned with their hardhearted leaders, yet true to the essence of their religions. As yet they have had little effect on leaders and institutions. It may be that many of them have more in common with each other than with some of their co-religionists: perhaps the generous-hearted and enlightened Sufi, for example, can be at home in Jewish spirituality, and their dialogue, separated from the polarizations of Middle Eastern politics, could in the long term be important.

I am painfully aware of gaps and over-simplifications in my treatment of this enormous subject, but I hope that the least I have done is to show that (in the words of Professor Ellis Rivkin, an American Jewish historian writing in 1979): 'The differences setting Islam apart from Judaism do not always generate hostility'.

REFERENCES

Ahmad, B. (1979) Muhammad and the Jews. A Re-examination, Vikas , New Delhi
Crone, P. and Cook, M. (1977) Hagarism. The Making of the Islamic World, Cambridge University Press
Ginzberg, L. (1909) Legends of the Bible, Philadelphia, repr. 1975
Goitein, S.D. (1974) Jews and Arabs. Their Contacts through the Ages, 3rd revised edition, Schocken Books, New York
Graetz, H. (1894) History of the Jews, Philadelphia
Guillaume, A. (1927) 'The Influence of Judaism on Islam' in E.R. Bevan and C. Singers (eds.), The Legacy of Israel, Oxford, pp.129-171
Lazarus Yafeh, H. (ed.) (1981) 'The sanctity of Jerusalem' in Religious Aspects of Islam. A Collection of Articles, E.J. Brill, Leiden, pp.58-71
Nemoy, L: (1956) 'Jews and Arabs', Jewish Quarterly Review, 46, pp.384-9
Rivkin, E. (1971) The Shaping of Jewish History, New York
Cantwell Smith, W. (1957) Islam in Modern History, Princeton
Watt, W.M. (1956) Muhammad at Medina, Oxford
Werblowsky, R.Z. (1976) Beyond Tradition and Modernity. Changing Religions in a Changing World, London

ISLAM AND THE FEMININE

R.W.J. Austin

At the present time, the world of Islam is reacting strongly to the mounting political, cultural and social pressures from the modern western world, in order to preserve its own traditional structures and identity, and the whole question of the status of women in contemporary Muslim society is becoming a major indicator as to the future success or otherwise of this Islamic revival. I feel that it is opportune, therefore, to explore in a general way, not only the question of the status and role of women in Islam, but also the question of the relationship between Islam as a patriarchal religious tradition and the whole phenomenon of the Feminine in human experience. As I hope to show later in this paper, such a· study is all the more relevant in view of certain new trends in feminist thinking, the implications of which strike at the very roots of the patriarchal tradition, Islamic or non-Islamic. I am, however, only too concious of the necessarily tentative and provisional nature of many of my suggestions and conclusions on this subject.

Before proceeding to the main part of the paper, it is necessary to define terms and to look more closely at the two subjects of the title, 'Islam' and the 'Feminine'. By Islam, I mean, of course that religious civilisation and community of faith established by the revelation of the Qur'an and shaped by the wisdom of the Prophet Muhammad as interpreted and transmitted to us by generations of the spiritually learned of that community. In particular, however, within the context of my subject today, I mean Islam as the last and most developed manifestation of the larger tradition of patriarchy. I do not think that anyone would dispute the fact that the religion of Islam is a part, not only of the Abrahamic monotheistic tradition of which Judaism and Christianity are also members, but also of a much larger tradition of patriarchal religion which includes most of the living religious traditions of our own time. It is this particular and very important aspect of Islam with which we must here be concerned, since it is in its patriarchal nature that its relationship with the Feminine is determined. Being patriarchal in its nature, Islam is therefore also androcentric and androcratic which implies, in actual terms, an inevitably secondary and satellite role for woman and what is feminine within the structure of its theology and society.

It is most important that the patriarchal principal and its implications for all the major living religious traditions be recognised and understood, since that nature underlies and informs a whole galaxy of associated explicit and implicit principles, values, imperatives and attitudes which, in different ways, have shaped the various manifestations of patriarchy in human history. That principle requires certain conditions to flourish and, beyond a certain limit, cannot tolerate contrary forces and influences to affect its fundamental structures without the danger of disintegration. It is only natural therefore that the traditions based on that principle should order their human institutions in such a way as to maintain and preserve that principle.

It is also important to understand what patriarchy itself is. Patriarchy is based upon the principle of the dominance of the father over the mother with respect to the parentage of children and, by extension, the primacy of the male in human society, which primacy implies the subordination of the females. Furthermore, paternity itself can only be established with any degree of certainty in individual cases by the very strict control of female mate section, in the absence of which only maternity is sure. Thus the only way in which a father can establish his fatherhood is by firstly ensuring that his female mate has no relations with any other man, and then by recognising the offspring as his by a process of adoption and naming.

In view, therefore, of the uncertainty and ambiguity attached to physical paternity and the vulnerability of the male in the maternal context of life generation, the principle of individual paternity could only assert its dominance on a basis other than that of the physical life cycle of which the female is the primary representative. That basis could only be the head-oriented principle of individual identity and separative consciousness, the 'I' as opposed to 'them', the subject which seeks to know and possess the object - which principle is given expression and identified by name and speech, which expresses its ideas and decisions by words (logoi) and which makes sense of and abstracts the 'other', the world, in verbal and mental formulations (logic). In order to survive and transcend the tyranny of physical death this principle must perpetuate itself through memory, again expressed by words, whether through oral or literal transmission, from one generation to the next. Furthermore, the suprahuman or divine is seen primarily in terms of an absolute identity-consciousness with an immutable, eternal and inalienable identity, who is always, significantly, called He.

Islam and the Feminine

Because this principle is an individual one, separating and isolating itself from the undifferentiated symbiotic experience of the female dominated collective, it tends also to be exclusive, competitive and, ultimately unique and single in its aspiration(1). Thus the patriarchal religious traditions are characterised in their higher forms by a preoccupation with identity-consciousness, name, word, spirit, intellect, truth and unity. They are more concerned with the hereafter than with this world, with the intangible that the sensible, with the ideal than the actual, with recorded history rather than myth, with what the mind believes and knows than with what the body feels and experiences. In all such traditions, woman, regarded as the representative of the earth-life pole, is, in fact, if not in theory, seen as a threat to the continuing detachment of this principle, except as fulfilling a subordinate and supportive role. Accordingly, they give all the dominant functions in religion and society to males and exclude females from areas regarded as specially sacred. Indeed, in their more intensive, mystical manifestations they become world-negating and thus feminine rejecting, as shown by the ideal of the hermit. Thus, in addition to its positive aspect in championing the principle of individual consciousness in human experience, many of its attitudes are shaped also by the need to resist forces contrary to patriarchal aspirations.

By the Feminine, I mean not only the sphere of the human woman, but also that whole complex of life-body experience of the natural cosmos of which the human female is the natural symbol, focus and representative, in which she is naturally dominant and which the patriarchy is so keen to limit and control.

It is a world of experience in which magic plays a greater part than logic, in which myth is more relevant than history, in which the tangible and visible are more effective transmitters of the sacred than the verbal and intellectual, in which the cosmic is seen as a tissue of mutually interrelated aspects rather than as a collection of separate entities, and in which the divine is seen more in terms of the womb than of the head. Its concerns are psycho-physical rather than mental-intellectual, communal rather than individual, vital rather than spiritual, with wholeness rather than with perfection and with the actual rather than the ideal. Much of what we know of the pre-history and early history of man's religious experience, in Europe, the Mediterranean littoral, the Middle East and India, is conveyed to us in the powerful feminine images of fertility and chthonic rites(2).

This then is the dimension of human experience which patriarchal religion seeks so carefully to supress and control. Indeed, every major patriarchal tradition is constantly affected at the grass roots by this alternative perspective since each such religion feels the need, periodically, to purge itself of such influences by 'reformation', 'revival' or 'renewal'(3).

Thus, although the non-patriarchal world-view may have been severely limited through milennia of patriarchal ascendancy, its past power looms like a shadow in the background, its influences are continuously seeping into the less completely converted lower reaches of patriarchal society, and it always threatens once more to claim the devotion of man and dissolve the magisterium of verbal-identity authority, as it seems, to many, to be succeeding in doing in modern western society. I have termed this alternative world-view, with all its religious, cultural, political and social implications, the Feminine, because it is the image of the divine Feminine which has, in the past, most completely given expression to it throughout the world(4).

In applying this scheme to the particular relationship, Islam and the Feminine, I have divided my paper into three parts. The first part concerns the way in which elements of the sacred Feminine present in pre-Islamic history lie, anonymously, so to speak, in the background of Islamic symbolism. In the second part, I examine the fundamental attitudes of Islam to the Feminine in its approach to women within its own system. Lastly, I will seek to explain why modern values and attitudes pose such a threat to the survival of the Islamic tradition, which is why the Islamic world is not reacting so strongly to any increase of modern influence; and also to explore important implications for the future of Islam of certain trends in feminist thinking which seek to revive interest in the divine Feminine.

Part One

Although each patriarchal tradition strives to suppress the dominant or divine Feminine by associating it with death and evil, and also to isolate its human representative, woman, from it by subordinating her roles to patriarchal goals and aspirations, the sacred Feminine can never properly be obliterated from human experience, but only consigned to a shadow role whose influences are often regarded as malefic. The sacred Feminine often also re-emerges within the patriarchal context almost in a compensatory role, often associated with manifestations of popular devotion. The most important example of this is the almost overwhelming re-emergence of the sacred Feminine in the cult of Mary in Christianity(5). In India also the sacred Feminine continues to exert enormous religious influence(6).

In Islam, which is the latest patriarchal tradition and which appeared on the scene after the disintegration of the surviving mother cults, the sacred Feminine whether in its

shadow aspect or in its compensatory aspect, is almost
entirely implicit and only occasionally becomes explicit outside
the context of exoteric Sunni Islam in Shi^{c}i Islam and Sufism.
The dominant or divine Feminine does, however, feature quite
prominently in the pre-Islamic past of Arabia, in general, and
of Mecca and the Ka^{c}ba in particular. Thus, in absorbing
certain elements of pre-Islamic religiosity, notably in the
pilgrimage rites, albeit carefully purged and re-originated,
Islam inevitably assimilated, as part of its liturgical
apparatus, elements which cryptically retain strong symbolic
associations with the sacred Feminine.

The most important and significant of these is at the
very heart of Islamic ritual and symbolism, namely the Ka^{c}ba
and its black stone at Mecca. As far as Islam is concerned its
use of the Ka^{c}ba represents only the restoration of a sacred
site, originally devoted to God and Abraham and only later
alienated to pagan use during the Jahiliyya or 'time of
ignorance'. According to Islam, therefore, the Ka^{c}ba is a
purely patriarchal site. However, it was certainly, for a
period, a polytheistic pantheon prominent in which was the
goddess al-^{c}Uzza and her consort god Hubal(7). In fact,
this goddess was one of three aspects of the Triple Goddess
celebrated wherever the goddess held sway, from Ireland to
India. Indeed, reference is made to her in the pages of the
Qur'an itself, albeit to deny her validity(8). These goddesses
were worshipped as virgin-mothers, virgin not in the
patriarchal sense as virgo intacta, but in the sense that
whatever their relations with gods or men, they remained, in
their divinity, unpossessed and self-sufficient.

In particular, it is a special association of the virgin
goddess with the Ka^{c}ba itself that I wish now to examine.
Although relatively little research has been done on this, and
although I am concious of treading, academically speaking, on
very thin ice, I would like, tentatively, to suggest that the
very concept and indeed nomenclature of the Ka^{c}ba was, at
some stage, specifically associated with the cult of a virgin
goddess, indeed that what the term Ka^{c}ba might have meant,
in pagan times, was what in Athens was called the Parthenon,
since the root of the word Ka^{c}ba, k^{c}b, means, primarily, to
mature physically (of a maiden), the related word ku^{c}ba
meaning virginity(9). In its primary sense it means the same
as the Greek word orgao which is probably the origin of the
Latin word virgo(10). In this connection it is interesting that
Epiphanius, writing of Nabatean religion, refers to al-Lat the
goddess mother of the Nabatean god, Dhu'l-Shara, as
Khaabou(11), and, more often than not, the goddess shrines
of the Arab tribes, called also Ka^{c}ba, consisted of massive
stones embedded in the earth, notably that of al-Lat at
Taif(12). Another curious piece of evidence for the
association is that a certain Zuhair ibn Ghanab ibn Hubal
referred to the Ka^{c}ba of the Ghatafan as an ^{c}adhra' or

virgin(13). Whatever the case may be, the indications as to such an association are more than just tenuous. They are reinforced to some extend by further assocations, in the ancient Middle East, between the black stone or meteorite and the worship of the goddess, notably the worship of Cybele(14).
Lesser indications are also to be found which suggest the shadow presence of the sacred Feminine, behind the veil, in Islam. It is quite possible, for example, that the practice of fasting in the month of Ramadan is related to the ancient practice, in Mesopotamia, of fasting for a period during the hottest month of the year in mourning for Tammuz the dead fertility-god and consort of the goddess Ishtar, the root meaning of the word ramadan being 'to be very hot or scorching'(15). Also the traditional symbol of Sunni Islam, the crescent moon and star, probably of Ottoman origin, was always, in ancient times, associated with the mysteries of the goddess.
All of this is not to say that Islam is not monotheistic or patriarchal, but only to illustrate that, like all other religious traditions which have emerged in history, it cannot completely suppress the non-patriarchal element. Indeed, there is much in Islam, as also in Christianity and Judaism, in the form of contra-feminine attitudes, which indicates how well aware Islam was and still is of the gynocentric religious potential deeply underlying its own structures.

Part Two

Within the context of the Islamic religious tradition itself, its relationship with the Feminine is almost entirely confined to its relations with the female members of its own community, since most vestiges of the goddess cults had been effectively obliterated by the time Islam appeared. In this sense, Islam is, perhaps, the most confident of the patriarchal religions in its patriarchal certainty, in that its androcentric monotheism has suffered none of the Feminine resurgences experienced in Christianity, and there is no trace in Islam of the religious matrilineality present in Judaism. Thus, inheriting as it does the age-old attitudes of patriarchal dominance, Islam fulfills the patriarchal mission in removing all trace from its own community of the connection between woman and the Divine.
Thus, we may observe in the relationship Islam - Feminine, within its own context, evidence of two trends, the one negative, reflecting its awareness of the latent sacred Feminine and its threat to the principle upon which patriarchy is based, the other positive, reflecting its confidence in dealing with the human female as being weak, passive and

obedient. The former approach is most evident in Islam in the theory of the shari^{c}a, the religious Law, and in the actualities of its dealings with women in the community, while the latter attitude is more evident in the Qur'an, the life of the 'Prophet and in the utterances of certain mystics, in other words at the ideal and spiritual pole of Islamic experience.

From previous patriarchal traditions it inherited the main imperatives essential to the survival of the patriarchy, namely the need to direct female mate selection, to ensure certainty of individual paternity, and to restrict the erotic power of woman to influence men, except to produce children. Thus, contact with a menstruating woman is strictly prohibited, partly because it is an infertile period and partly because menstruation has perennially been associated with women's mysteries(16). Veiling or covering of the female body is commanded, partly to reduce erotic influences and partly to prevent unstipulated relations(17). Pork and wine are forbidden, the first because of its very strong associations with the earlier goddess cults, as a sacred animal, the second, because it impairs the quality of consciousness and identity, so important a feature of patriarchal spirituality(18).

Thus, in Islam we find a certain tension between a higher patriarchal idealism regarding women, and the lower patriarchal need to control the situation on the ground. In the first case, as in other such traditions, woman is idealised and seen as the beautiful and passive mirror of Truth, ever sensitive to the higher aspirations of man, while in the second case, woman in all her roles and functions is an ever present reality demanding, cajoling, influencing and attracting, whom Muslim man must needs control.

On the one hand, the Qur'an clearly recognises the spiritual equality of man and woman as human beings subject to God and encourages kind and just treatment of women, except where they threaten serious disobedience(19), just as the Prophet, throughout his life, loved and respected women and treated them very well(20). The Qur'an accords woman far more rights and privileges than were enjoyed by Christian women until the 19th century, and Muslim women are, in Law, as much citizens as men, with certain disadvantages. Many mystics, among them the celebrated Jalal al-Din Rumi and Ibn al-^{c}Arabi, extol the ideal of spiritual womanhood, and see in the feminine a symbol, not only of receptive Universal Nature, but also of the divine mystery itself(21). These very positive attitudes, however, are inspired by an archetype of ideal womanhood, particularly in its maternal aspect, which is epitomised, in the Qur'an, by the figure of Mary, the mother of Jesus(22). There she is a perfect example of the ^{c}ubudiyya or servant aspect of the human relationship with God, the aspect of khilafa or viceregency being represented by the male. This picture of supportive motherhood, devoted womanhood and truth-reflecting beauty is, however, an ideal image. The other side of the coin is indicated in the Qur'an by the words, musafihat and muttakhidhat akhdhan, the first meaning a promiscuous woman, the second term meaning those women who take lovers, in other words those women who defy patriarchal controls and feel free to choose how and with whom they may have sexual relations(23). Clearly, this type of freedom constitutes, potentially, a grave threat to the very principles upon which patriarchal religious tradition is based, so that it cannot be tolerated and must be severely punished. Thus, in Islam, illicit sexual relations, outside the pattern laid down by the Law, is one of those offenses which are seen, not as an offense against man, but against God, in that they strike at the very roots of patriarchal ascendancy(24). Thus, when a woman seeks an illicit lover she has sought to put herself beyond the control and right of whatever male has charge of her. Indeed, the rebellious and defiant woman is regarded as a serious threat to be punished by beating, solitary confinement and, ultimately, death(25). In fact, as in other patriarchal cultures, the woman, despite her human-spiritual equality with man, is thought of only in terms of her relationship to some man.

Indeed, the woman who is confident and seeks to use her power over men in taking the initiative is seen most of all as the representative of that elemental feminine power to condition and dissolve which the Muslim religious establishment has always feared, condemned and denigrated, which has resulted in the fact that, in contrast to the stipulations and spirit of the Qur'an and Prophetic example, women in the history of the Muslim society have been treated more strictly and allowed less scope than the letter of the Law permits(26). This is because, despite male confidence, there is always the underlying awareness of the potential of the Feminine to break down patriarchal order and certainty and to re-assert its dominance, all of which is often seen as confirming a special relationship between the Feminine and Satan. A tradition of the Prophet states that Satan rejoiced when woman was created(27), just as Christian monks once spoke of woman as the way in for the Devil, all of which indicates that, at a certain level, women were regarded, as fickle, unreliable, sensual and at the mercy of their feelings, their attractive power making them even more an object of caution and anxiety(28).

Outside the question of the status of women in Islamic society, there are also certain Islamic concepts and symbols with positive feminine connotations which serve further to illustrate the Islamic view of the role and function of the Feminine in the divine scheme of things. Most important of these is the Muslim notion of the community of faith, in Arabic al-umma, a word closely related to the word umm meaning mother. Thus the Muslim community is seen, in its relationship with God, as essentially receptive, open to receive the deposition of the Divine Word. Thus, the receptive community is seen as the human image of the primordial receptivity of universal nature. Very closely related to this symbolism is the Prophet's own spiritual receptivity to the inflow of divine revelation, seeing that he is called ummi, translated as 'illiterate', or in other words untainted by human 'word', and thus ready to be receptive to His word. Thus, the Prophet Muhammad, in the verbal sense, fulfills much the same role in Islam as does Mary, in the physical sense, in Christianity.

Finally, in Shi͟ᶜi Islam, the daughter of the Prophet, Fatima, as wife to ᶜAli and mother to their sons, Hasan and Husain, assumes a greater devotional significance, as mother of a holy family, than would be possible in Sunni Islam where the Feminine, in any aspect, is largely veiled and implicit.

Thus, in Islam, the Qur'an, the Sunna, the Law, and the history of Muslim religious tradition and social values we may observe a very clear tension and often conflict between an ideal image of the feminine, and between a more immediate contact with the feminine in the actual ordering of human society where the potential threat of the Feminine to patriarchal values is an actual experience, reinforced by the collective memory of the power of the now rapid decline and disintegration of patriarchal structures and values in the modern Western world.

Part Three

Islam has, in the past few years, having largely recovered from the trauma of physical conquest and occupation, been directing its energies more and more to understanding and resisting whereever possible the on-going effects of social and cultural colonialism. This has been greatly increased by the political and economic decline of the West and the corresponding resurgence of certain Muslim states due to the accumulation of oil wealth. In addition, increasing western style education among the Muslim elite has enabled many to understand what is happening in western society, to appreciate the extent to which Muslim societies were becoming second-rate copies of western societies, and to realise more fully the need to rediscover and reassert their own political, social and cultural identity, which -- given the apparent ineffectiveness of the formula -- means, today, Islamic identity.

This growing rediscovery of identity has revealed what is perhaps the greatest significant difference between the concept of religion in the once Christian West and in the world of Islam. While Christianity has never properly been a religion of the mundane state and is very suited to being, as it was in its early phase, a religion of private individual commitment, Islam sees religion as including all aspects of human activity, individual and collective, the state as well as the church, the sensual as well as the spiritual. Therefore, any attempt to reduce Islam to the private sphere or to restrict it to purely devotional and spiritual concerns is rightly seen as an attempt to de-nature Islam, to make it only part of itself. Islamic revival does not mean, to Muslims, only religious revival, but also political, social and cultural renewal. Furthermore such renewal does not mean the reformation or altering of Islamic structures, but rather, as we now see in Iran and Saudi Arabia, the restoration of original and traditional patterns and the elimination of alien influences.

This being the case, Islamic revival means in effect, in the context of our theme, the strengthening and restoration of values and structures that are unambiguously patriarchal, which inevitably means the elimination or restriction of any social or political influences from outside Islam which threaten such structures. In most Muslim countries where the process of renewal and elimination is vigorous, one of the most important manifestations of stopping the rot has been to halt the western inspired process of female emancipation and to reinstate with great zeal the segregation of the sexes, the veiling and restriction of women in public and the purging of the media of all sexually provocative material. It seems that Muslims have realised, if only unconsciously, that the question of the status, freedom and scope of women to influence society directly or not is perhaps the most crucial one for the survival of Muslim patterns of society and thus for Islam as a whole, and that any significant dilution of patriarchal norms in this respect could only result in the irreparable alteration of what Islam and its community are meant to be.

In many ways modern western society is now a non- and, in certain respects, an anti-partriarchal society which is concerned with and committed to experiences and goals quite other than those of the patriarchal religious traditions, as Christianity has discovered to its cost.

It should be clear from this, therefore, that the world of Islam, dedicated as it is to patriarchal values, and relatively unaffected, except from outside its own traditional context by contra-patriarchal developments, cannot, if it is to survive as Islam, the religion-state, permit any increase of western influences, particularly social and cultural. Perhaps fortunately for Islam, the greater mass of its believers remain, even today, relatively unaffected by the profounder implications of western developments and, one might say, not at all by any experience of Rennaisance or Reformation within their own context.

As has already been indicated, a significant, if not the most significant, part of the threat posed by the modern world for Islam is the question of the status and freedom of action of women and the degree to which they are permitted to wield their influence, in all its aspects, in society, since on the answer to that question rests, inescapably, the survival of the whole fabric of patriarchal civilisation. Indeed, one must say ultimately that Islam, as a patriarchal tradition cannot afford to permit to women anything but a supportive and confirmative role in its society, nor can it, realistically, tolerate any development within its society which is likely to lead to a substantial increase of feminine power.

Significantly, in this respect there is a growing interest in the West, at many levels, in the notion of the sacred and divine Feminine and the restoration of female consciousness of feminine mysteries relating to the whole cycle of female natural experience. Indeed, certain feminist groups are now speaking of the revival and re-discovery of the Goddess religions, and many books of various kinds, archaeological, historical and psychological have been published on this and related subjects in recent times(29). Furthermore, much of the recent interest in the re-discovery of the sacred Feminine goes together with a corresponding attempt to disparage the whole patriarchal tradition and accuse it of the usurpation of Feminine divinity.

It must be quite clear that this last development is one which Islam cannot tolerate, seeing that it seeks to undermine and relativise the very principle of absolutity and spiritual principle upon which the patriarchal traditions are founded, Islamic or otherwise. The suggestion, now being made in certain quarters, that patriarchal monotheism postdates and develops from the religion of the goddess, is one which Islam, and all other such religions, must perforce reject and eradicate, unless the whole edifice of revealed truth and doctrine is not to come toppling down, as has partially happened in the West for the majority, and patriarchal religion become merely an interesting part of our cultural heritage or an ideological support institution for famine relief and popular liberation movements.

The future of Islam, therefore, as Islam, must lie in its determination, whatever outside pressures be brought to bear, to maintain the patriarchal structures and values which alone can sustain the doctrinal principles on which monotheism claims to be founded.

NOTES

1. Cf. Neumann, E., The Origins and History of Consciousness (Princeton, 1970), p.340 ff.

2. James, E.O., The Tree of Life (Leiden, 1966), p.161.
3. Cf. Cohn, N., Europe's Inner Demons (London, 1975).
4. James, Tree of Life, Chapter 6.
5. Cf. Ashe, G., The Virgin (London, 1976).
6. Cf. Maury, K., Folk Origins of Indian ·Art (Columbia University Press, 1969).
7. Fahd, T., Le Pantheon de l'Arabie Centrale a la Veille de l'Hegire (Paris, 1968), p.163 ff.
8. Qur'an, 53: 19-23.
9. Lane, E.W., Arabic-English Lexicon (London, 1867), art. k^{c}b.
10. Liddell and Scott, Greek - English Lexicon (Oxford, 1901), art. orgao; Lewis and Short, Latin Dictionary (Oxford, 1900), art. virgo.
11. Fahd, Pantheon, p.204.
12. Ibid., p.111.
13. Ibid., p.171 ff.
14. James, Tree of Life, p.186 ff.
15. Lane, Lexicon, art. rmd.
16. Qur'an, 2:222. Cf. Shuttle, P. and Redgrove, P., The Wise Wound (London, 1978), Chaps. 4 and 5.
17. Qur'an, 24:31.
18. Ibid., 5:3 and 91.
19 Ibid., 4:19.
20. Ibn Hisham, Life of Muhammad, trans. Guillaume, A. (Oxford, 1955), p.651.
21. Cf. Jalal al-Din Rumi Mathnawi, ed. and trans. Nicholson, R.A., vol. 1 (London, 1925-40), p.2431. Corbin, H., Creative Imagination in the Sufism of Ibn ^{c}Arabi (London, 1971), chap. 2.
22. Qur'an, 66:12.
23. Ibid., 4:25.
24. Ibid., 2:187.
25. Ibid., 4:15.
26. Cf. Al-Bukhari, M., Al-sahih (Cairo, 1953), 67:17.
27. Ibid.
28. Qur'an, 24:31.
29. Shorter Encyclopaedia of Islam (London, 1961), art. Fatima.
30. Cf. Shuttle and Redgrove, Wise Wound; Stone, M., The Paradise Papers (London, 1976); Davis, E., The First Sex (London, 1975).

REFERENCES

Ashe, G. (1976) The Virgin, London
Al-Bukhari, M. (1953) Al-sahih, Cairo
Cohn, N. (1975) Europe's Inner Demons, London
Corbin, H. (1971) Creative Imagination in the Sufism of Ibn

^cArabi, London

Davis, E. (1975) The First Sex, London

Fahd, T. (1968), Le Pantheon de l'Arabie Centrale a la Veille de l'Hegire, Paris

Gibb, H.A.R. and Kramers, J.H. (eds.) (1961) Shorter Encyclopaedia of Islam, London

Ibn Hisham (1955) Life of Muhammad, trans. Guillaume, A., Oxford

James, E.O. (1966) The Tree of Life, Leiden

Maury, K. (1969) Folk Origins of Indian Art, Columbia University Press

Neumann, E. (1970) The Origins and History of Consciousness, Princeton

Rumi, Jalal al-Din (1925-40) Mathnawi, ed. and trans. Nicholson, R.A., 8 vols., London

Shuttle, P. and Redgrove, P. (1978) The Wise Wound, London

Stone, M. (1976) The Paradise Papers, London

SUFISM AND PSEUDO-SUFISM

L. P. Elwell-Sutton

In recent years in the West there has been a spate of new religious movements, many of them claiming to draw their inspiration from eastern sources. Among these perhaps none have attracted as much attention as the various movements that claim for themselves the designation of Sufism. It is difficult sometimes to judge such movements. The kind of questions one must ask are: Do these movements have anything to say to the West? Have they a role to play in modern Islamic society?

Before one can answer such questions, one must be satisfied that they are indeed authentic Sufi movements, for like other religious movements trying to root themselves in alien soil, alien in either place or time, they are likely to attract frauds and charlatans ever ready to exploit the credulous. To answer such doubts, we must first take a hard look at the origins and nature of Sufism in its own environment, that of early Islam.

For one point must be made clear from the start. Sufism is an Islamic movement, and to become a true Sufi one must first become a Muslim and subject one's self to the full range of Islamic doctrine and teaching. Only then can one 'specialise', by penetrating through the facade of orthodoxy to the deeper truths that lie behind.

Now, since a number of 'western' pseudo-Sufi teachers implicitly deny this principle by ignoring it, it is necessary to look at it a little more closely. Can the teachings of Sufism be justified by reference to the Qur'an, the fountain of all Islamic doctrine? Certainly Sufism appears to have much in common with other mystical movements, in that it aims at an intuitive, spiritual awareness of God, achieved by direct experience, not by the intellect. At that level there is no difference between Islamic, Christian, Judaic or any other mysticism. But this is not really what is at issue. It is not the end result that we are concerned with, but the means by which it is achieved, and it is here that the differences arise.

The term Sufism can only be applied to the brand of mysticism that developed in Islam. Even the name is Arabic. Dismissing the fanciful derivations offered by some adherents, both ancient and modern, who were seeking a more dignified etymology, we can have no doubt that the word comes from the Arabic suf, wool, and refers to the woollen garments (equivalent to the monkish hair-shirt) worn by early Muslim asctics (zuhhad). The Persian equivalent, though of much later date - pashmina-push, 'wool-wearer' - makes this quite clear. The first recorded use of the name Sufi was applied to a certain Abu Hashim of Kufa, who died in 767. The term tasawwuf, meaning the practice of the Sufi life, or tout court Sufism, is attributed to the 8th century mystic Ma^cruf al-Karkhi.

So we are talking about a term that made its first recorded appearance some 150 years after the revelation of the Qur'an to the Prophet Muhammad. Yet there is no question but that true Sufism draws its inspiration and much of its vocabulary from the Qur'an. The earliest form was pure asceticism, self-denying devotion to God, arising out of an exaggerated consciousness of sin and dread of Divine retribution. Indeed the idea that God can be known by man directly is still rejected in orthodox Islamic circles, since according to their view communion is possible only between like and like, and man can never be equal to God. The Qur'an itself is open to interpretation on this point. It is not clear that the Prophet himself ever claimed to have spoken with God; the Qur'an, though the Word of God, was revealed to him by the angel Gabriel. The expression used in the Qur'an to refer to the bearer of the revelation, 'Then came he nearer and approached and was at the distance of two bows, or even nearer' (53:8-9), which the orthodox regard as applying to Gabriel, is taken, however, by the Sufis as referring to God. Another expression much quoted by Sufis is 'We (i.e. God) are closer to him (man) than his jugular vein'(50:16); while the account of Muhammad's Night Journey, 'Glory be to Him Who carried his servant by night from the sacred temple to the temple that is more remote...that We might show him of Our signs' (17:1), has been built up in subsequent Sufi lore to an elaborate account of the Prophet's ascent through the seven heavens until he found himself in the presence of God and received commands from Him. Such Qur'anic statements, as well as hadiths, sayings of the Prophet and his Companions, have been invoked by Sufis to justify their claim that man may have direct access to God.

But Sufism in its early days had not progressed as far as this. It is best summed up in the words attributed to Hasan al-Basri (643-728): 'He who is content, needing nothing, and who has sought solitude, apart from mankind, will find peace; he who has trodden his carnal desires underfoot, will find freedom; he who has rid himself of envy will find friendship, and he who has patience for a little while will find himself prepared for eternity'. (trans. Margaret Smith).

The first century or so of Islam, under the Umayyad Caliphs, was a period of gross materialism in high places, and it was a natural reaction to turn towards an unworldly life, to seek refuge in retreat from the material world. By the middle of the eight century we hear of the formation of 'monasteries' (khanqah, ribat, khalwa, zawiya), though at this stage they were still primarily hostels for itinerant mystics. However they provided the setting for a more organised monastic life.

It is during the ninth century that the direction of Sufism begins to change. The practice of asceticism in its more extreme forms led to spiritual experiences that could only be understood as insights into a more real world behind the surface of the known material world. Thus Ma⁽ᶜ⁾ruf al-Karkhi said: 'Sufism is to grasp the verities (al-haqa'iq) and to renounce that which is in the hands of men'. Possibly under the influence of neo-Platonism (though all talk of influences of this kind should be taken with a pinch of salt) developed the principles of ma⁽ᶜ⁾rifa, knowledge of the real behind the facade; tawhid, awareness of the unity of God and His creation; and mahabba, yearning for the presence of God. The following quotations from Dhu'l-Nun al-Misri (796-861) illustrate these:

Tawhid: O God, I never hearken to the voices of the beasts or the rustle of the trees, the splashing of waters or the song of birds, the whistling of the wind or the rumble of thunder, but I sense in them a testimony to Thy Unity (trans. A.J. Arberry).

Ma⁽ᶜ⁾rifa: The gnostics see without knowledge, without sight, without information received, and without observation, without description, without veiling and without veil. They are not themselves, but in so far as they exist at all, they exist in God. (trans. Margaret Smith).

Mahabba: The saints are those whom God has invested with the radiance of His love, and adorned with the fair mantle of His grace, upon whose heads he set the crown of His joy, and He put love towards them into the hearts of His creatures. (trans. Margaret Smith).

From this point Sufism develops along two main, but not necessarily contradictory, streams of thought: the 'western', represented by the Iraqi Junaid (d.910), in which stress was laid on sobriety, observance of the shari⁽ᶜ⁾a (the Holy Law), striving to reach God through piety and reliance of Him. Man, it was claimed, originally existed in God; his separate

51

existence was the consequence of a deliberate act of God's will. The Qur'an says: 'He hath created the Heavens and the Earth to set forth His truth' (16:3; cf. 10:5). A Sufi hadith qudsi (a non-Qur'anic saying attributed to God) says: 'I was a hidden treasure, and I wanted to be known, so I created man that I might be known'. The Qur'an also speaks of God's covenant with man before creation:"Am I not', said He, 'your Lord?' They said, 'Yes, we witness it'. This We did, lest ye should say on the Day of Resurrection, 'Truly, of this we were heedless, because uniformed'....Thus We make Our signs clear; that haply they may return to God". So man's duty is to fulfil that covenant, to seek to return to God. Through Sufism God causes man to die to himself (fana') and to live in God (baqa').

The 'eastern' stream, influenced perhaps by Hinduism and Buddhism (but see the caveat above), of whom the most notable representatives were Abu Yazid Bistami (d. 874) and the probably legendary Ibrahim ibn Adham, whose life-story bears a striking resemblance to that of the Buddha, is marked by its emphasis on ecstasy and 'intoxication' (wajd, sukr). Abu Yazid thus describes his mi'raj or ascent to Heaven (a term previously only used of the Prophet's Night Journey):

> And when God Most-Glorious perceived the sincerity of my desire to seek Him, He called to me and said: 'O My chosen one, approach unto me and ascend to the heights of My glory and the plains of My splendour and sit upon the carpet of My holiness, so that thou mayest see the working of My grace in My appointed time...' Then I began to melt away, as lead melts in the heat of the fire. Then He gave me to drink from the fountain of grace in the cup of fellowship and changed me into a state beyond description and brought me near unto Him...I continued thus until I became even as the souls of men had been, in that state before existence was and God abode in solitude apart... (trans. Margaret Smith).

A further development along the lines set down by Bistami was the movement of the Malamatiyya, the Blameworthy Ones, who in furtherance of the rejection of self concealed their piety and good actions from other people, and even deliberately attempted to attract the condemnation of the world by rejecting the requirements of the shari'a, the public performance of prayers and ritual, and so on. In the case of some of the later dervish groups this led to a tendency to overstep the bounds of propriety, stressing that ethical virtues, worldly morality, had nothing to do with the spiritual pilgrimage. Man, they said, is as nothing in comparison with God, and his actions therefore worthless. Husain ibn Mansur al-Hallaj (d. 922), addressing God, exclaimed, 'If Thou wert to offer to sell me Paradise for a moment of my time with Thee...I would not buy it. If Thou wert to place before me Hell-fire...J would think lightly of it in comparison with my state when Thou art hidden from me...Do with me what Thou wilt'. (Trans. Margaret Smith).

It was al-Hallaj who uttered what seemed to the orthodox to be the ultimate blasphemy, and for which he paid with his life: 'If ye do not recognise God, at least recognise His signs. I am that sign, I am the Truth (ana 'l-Haqq), because through the Truth I am a truth eternally'. Hallaj was not of course claiming to be God, as his opponents thought, but that he was so insignificant as to have no existence apart from God.

Sufism up to this time was primarily a personal matter, but there were the beginnings of group activity, with bands of disciples gathered round a Master to learn from him the Way (tariqa). At the same time, and in response to the same demands, Sufi doctrine was becoming formalised. The Way was being mapped out. Systems of maqamat (stages) and halat (mystic states) were worked out, through which the seeker must pass in order to attain the ultimate. Personal effort was necessary, subject to the guidance of a murshid (guide), but the receptive soul might also receive gifts of vision from God. The chosen few might achieve both ma^{c}rifa (gnosis) and wilaya (sainthood) without following a Path.

There is not space here to discuss in detail the later developments in Sufi doctrine and theosophy: al-Insan al-Kamil, the concept of the Perfect Man, the prototype of the universe and of man; al-Nur al-Muhammadiyya, the Muhammadan Light, the first thing created by God, of which the world is a manifestation; the invisible hierarchy of saints (awliya'), headed by the Pole (Qutb) of his Time; the role played by the mysterious figure of al-Khadir or Khizr, said to have originally been Moses' murshid and the repository of esoteric knowledge (al-^{c}ilm al-ladunni), referred to in the Qur'an (18:64-65); Suhrawardi's hikmat al-ishraq (illuminism, philosophy of light); Ibn al-^{c}Arabi's doctrine of wahdat al-wujud - all things pre-exist as ideas in the knowledge of God, whence they emanate and whither they ultimately return.

Side by side with these developments went, after a period of savage persecution, a move towards respectability and institutionalisation. The twelfth century marked the beginning of the foundation of Sufi orders, usually taking their name form their founder. Over the centuries many such orders came into being, while others split up or disappeared. But the pattern for all of them was similar. They were based on the silsila or isnad - the transmission of esoteric doctrine, rules and methods through a chain of adepts who have undergone the full course of training and have received manifestations of Divine Grace. Usually such chains are traced back to the Prophet, but it is rarely a matter of hereditary succession in a family, rather a matter of each shaikh in turn nominating his successor by some symbolic gesture.

Thus transmitted knowledge is now superseding personal experience, and authority - the authority of hadith or the current shaikh - becomes the guiding force. There is stress on ritual tasks - dhikr, the repetition of the Names of God, of verses from the Qur'an, of prayers, of Sufi and especially Persian poetry. Other practices, frowned on by the orthodox, became popular - music, dancing, drugs, the contemplation of handsome youths (for although there were female Sufis, in general it was a male activity). Ecstasy became the end, instead of a means to a more profound destination. At the level of popular religion particularly, these aspects became more important than the original spirituality of the early Sufis. Some adherents rebelled against these formalistic aspects to follow the dervish life, casting aside conventional behaviour and morality in a revolt reminiscent of the Malamatiyya of earlier centuries.

All this serves to underline the fissiparous nature of Sufism. It is not a single unchanging body of teaching handed down by secret word of mouth and reserved for the fully initiated, but an historical development of religious and mystical doctrines, experiences and practices, taking many different forms in different parts of the Islamic world at different points in time. It was the orders, needing to attract adherents, who played on the meretricious fascination of the promise of a secret esoteric doctrine to be revealed to the initiate in due course. But the fact, of course, is that there is no such sercret teaching. The stages of the Way can be and have been described in words. But the experiences themselves can only be known by actually traversing the Path through all its stages, and few have achieved this. To do so demands complete surrender and abandonment of all else to a single-minded way of life. It certainly cannot be learnt by a few weeks' meditation in the Himalayas, or a weekend on a country estate in Kent.

Yet unfortunately it is precisely these spurious and negative aspects of 'popular' Sufism that are being exploited by bogus 'masters' in the West, often sporting oriental-sounding names. Such persons play on the doubts and fears of lost and bewildered intellectuals, fascinated by the lure of the 'mysterious east' and desperate for some ready-made solution to the disorder and chaos that they see around them. At the same time they cannot be pushed too far. Reared in a materialist environment, they cannot accept the notion of a spiritual force outside and above man and the material world. So Western pseudo-Sufi teachers are careful to omit all talk of God from their teaching, to base their prescriptions firmly on this world, and to avoid any suggestion of self-surrender to a transcendent Deity. Coupled to this are vague hints of secret knowledge garnered from remote corners of Asia (the remoter the better) that, once imparted, will set the initiate apart from his fellowmen. None of this requires even the rigorous training prescribed, if not always followed, by the Sufi orders, let alone the whole-hearted involvement in and surrender to the search for God that was the whole existence of the ancient Sufis.

Meanwhile in the Islamic homelands too Sufism is on a losing streak. Those governments and regimes who look to technological progress and modernisation as the essential route to survival in the modern world have no use for Sufism, which they charge with encouraging a negative, passive attitude to life, and in consequence being largely responsible for the decline of the Muslim peoples vis-a-vis their rivals in the West. In Kemalist Turkey the public practice of Sufi ritual was banned, and though in Pahlavi Iran the hostility was not so overt, Sufism and Sufi orders existed under a cloud. And quite apart from official disfavour, the educated, westernised elite adopted much the same attitude. Ironically, the atomosphere of repression that tends to be associated with such regimes was a powerful stimulus to the withdrawal from participation in public life that was so frowned on. In Iran during the later Pahlavi years Sufi orders flourished, drawing adherents from all walks of life.

Equally, however, Sufism was disliked by orthodox Islam. Perhaps this is particularly true in the Shi[c]i part of the Islamic world, especially Iran, where some of the attitudes, traditions and beliefs of the Sufis find their parallels in Shi[c]i lore. In consequence there has grown up a sense, not of fellowship, but of rivalry. The Shi[c]i divines seem almost to accuse the Sufis of poaching on their territory. There is little evidence coming out of Iran as to the fate of Sufism and Sufis under the Khumainist regime, but it seems unlikely that they are regarded with favour.

It could, therefore, be argued that Sufism no longer has a role to play. In both East and West it has travelled far from the spiritual sources out of which it grew, and has for the most part degenerated into a narrow, dessicated formalism. But if it teaches us no more than that man proposes but God disposes, it will not be altogether valueless. We already hear talk about the 'man-made future'; but if one thing is more certain than anything else, it is that, whoever does make the future, it is not man. Perhaps the Sufis - the true Sufis - can give us the answer.

REFERENCES

Arberry, A.J. (1950) Sufism, London
Attar, Farid al-Din (1966) Muslim Saints and Mystics, trans. A.J. Arberry, London, repr. 1979

Burckhardt, T. (1959) An Introduction to Sufi Doctrine, Lahore

Lings, Martin (1975) What is Sufism?, London

Nasr, S.H. (1966) Ideals and Realities of Islam, London, revd. 1971

Idem., (1972) Sufi Essays, London (reprinted as Living Sufism)

Rice, Cyprian (1964) The Persian Sufies, London

Schuon, F. (1962) Understanding Islam, London

Smith, Margaret (1950) Readings from the Mystics of Islam, London

SUFISM IN MODERN SUDAN(1)

Ahmed Al-Shahi

The purpose of this paper is three-fold: to discuss the introduction of Sufi orders into the Sudan and the beliefs and practices associated with them, then to consider the political participation of these orders, and finally to assess the position of these orders at the present-time. In so doing, I have relied on my own observations and research experience, and on published historical sources. I will confine the discussion to the Arab/Muslim people of northern Sudan: southern Sudanese, who were granted their regional autonomy in 1972, are non-Arab and non-Muslim with their own distinctive cultures and languages. However, political events and decisions by the central government in Khartoum have repercussions on the southern Sudanese people.

The Sudan encompasses tribal, linguistic, ecological and religious diversity. To cite one example of this diversity, the 1955-6 Census enumerated 597 tribes and 130 languages. In Sudan's recent political history a number of tribal movements have been formed in the west, east and south to speak for the political rights of particular tribal groups. These movements have been viewed by successive governments as a threat to the political stability and unity of the country. Nevertheless, it is essential that the diversity and distinctiveness of the Sudanese people be recognized and allowed expression if the political structure is not to be always under threat.

Furthermore, the Sudan has many neighbours: some are Muslim/Arabs but others are non-Arabs and non-Muslim with an Arab or Muslim minority. In its foreign policy the Sudan has to take into consideration its relationship with these neighbouring countries; recently its relationships have been unsettled and in some cases turbulent. The Sudan claims a stake in both the African and the Arab worlds in view of its geographical and cultural composition. Sudan's Arab connection has never been in doubt but the Sudanese cannot afford to ignore the feelings of the non-Arab and non-Muslim people who represent the African connection. Thus until recently its foreign policy took a moderate course not only towards Arab and African countries but also towards eastern and western countries.

One major feature of Sudan's internal politics has been the influence and dominance of sectarianism (ta'ifiyya) since the nineteenth century. This long established tradition of political involvement by religious orders reflects a continuing belief in and allegiance to sectarianism. Nationalist movements have incorporated differing religious groups, whether followers of Sufi orders or fundamentalists, in their drive for independence. Even members of the growing educated class, who advocate the secularity of politics, are either followers of Sufi orders or have allied themselves with these orders. The first national movement, the Mahdiyya, was religious in its motivation and it used religion as a pretext for political protest and action against the Turco-Egyptian rule (1821-1885).

The two major Sufi orders, the Mahdiyya (or Ansar) and the Khatmiyya, have sizeable followings in the country, with the exception of the Southern Region and the Nuba Hills, and in consequence have participated in politics and in government during periods of parliamentary rule. There are other minor Sufi orders with a limited following and of little political influence, e.g. Shadhiliyya, Qadiriyya, Sammaniyya, Tijaniyya, Majdhubiyya, Ahmadiyya, Idrisiyya, Rashidiyya, Isma'iliyya and Hindiyya. But before embarking on assessing the influence and viability of religious orders in the present-day Sudan, I would like to give a brief account of how Islam came to the country.

Immigrant men of religion spread Islam and Sufism in the Sudan, where some of them settled and established a following. Later, Sudanese men of religion founded Sufi orders which became specifically Sudanese and were confined to the Sudan(2). The Sudan never became part of the Arab or Islamic Empire. Despite the fact that an Arab/Muslim army unsuccessfully invaded the Christian Kingdom of Dongola in the seventh century, Islam and Arabism penetrated the country peacefully and gradually through migration, trade, the efforts of men of religion and intermarriage. This penetration effectively started from the fourteenth century onwards from two main areas: Arabia and Egypt. As a result of this penetration, Islam, the Arab tribal system and the Arabic language became firmly established among the inhabitants of the northern Sudan. The Sudd, in the south, formed an ecological barrier which the Arabs could not cross at that time, and hence the southern Sudanese maintained their own cultural traditions.

Immigrant and indigenous men of religion have profoundly shaped present-day Islam in the Sudan. These men of religion were received hospitably by the people and gradually acquired a religious reputation and a following. The

Islam brought by these men of religion was orthodoxy in the form of Sufi or mystical orders(3). Thus Sufism and the associated belief in the power of saints became an integral aspect of people's religious life. But the Sufism which became popular in the Sudan was at variance with that of the early mystics. To the true mystic or Sufi there is a need to satisfy the deeper longings of the soul which seeks a perfect communion with God. Through love a mystic achieves closeness with God and ultimately an identification with Him, the Divine Oneness. This state can be attained by living apart from the world, by contemplation and meditation, and by chanting praises and performing religious exercises which produce a state of ecstasy leading to union with God.

The Sufis of the Sudan would have been accused of heresy and polytheism, (shirk) by the non-Sufis if they had included in their teaching the concept of the Divine Oneness. Instead, they instructed their followers to concentrate on devotion and ascetic discipline. Spiritual devotion is made first to the head of the order, the shaikh, then to the Prophet Muhammad and finally to God. The followers of a particular Sufi order are expected to emulate the acts and prayers of the head of the order and to meditate upon him leading to the realization of the spiritual bond, love, between them and him. By practising these devotions, the followers will be spiritually transformed into the head of the order and then introduced, so to speak, through him to the Prophet(4) and ultimately to God. In this chain of spiritual hierarchy, grace, (baraka) is passed down from God to the followers through the Prophet, who is nearest to Him, and through the head of the order. These two are, therefore, intercessors between God and the followers of the order. This doctrine is not in contradiction with the belief in Islam that God is transcendant and unknowable.

Each founder of a Sufi order laid down certain rules concerning relationships between himself and his followers, wrote manuals, litanies and praises which the followers are expected to recite, and prescribed certain religious exercises. Once an individual has been initiated into the order he remains spiritually attached to the founder and his successors, and hence the continuity of spiritual bondage and allegiance. Sufism shares with orthodoxy the belief in and adherence to the five tenets of Islam (belief in one God and that Muhammad is His Prophet, the five daily prayers, fasting for the whole month of Ramadan, pilgrimage to the holy places, and giving alms to the poor) and the shari^{c}a or Islamic Law, which governs certain aspects of personal relationships such as marriage, divorce and inheritance. Adherence to the above are the requirements which should be observed by the followers of a Sufi order. To use a Sufi metaphor, the shari^{c}a is the root of the tree, tariqa or order is the branch, and the haqiqa or truth(the true nature of

God) is the fruit.

The crucial difference between Sufism and orthodoxy concerns the position of saints in Islam. The cult of saint veneration developed with the rise of Sufi orders in the twelfth century. Because of their piety, zeal and devotion, heads of Sufi orders claimed to have powers of intercession with God and to be able to perform miracles (karamat). Heads of Sufi orders are venerated and looked upon as holy-men, and their possession of grace stems from their being 'honoured' by God with His special favour. In other words grace is a gift given by God and the miracle of a shaikh is an honour. Because of their nearness to God and the powers they claim, shaikhs, dead or alive, are held in high esteem. Their names are called upon at times of illness, distress and danger. Their tombs are periodically visited to show reverence and in order to receive a share of grace. The common belief is that the saints' powers of intercession and performance of miracles are hereditary, which explains their association with certain religious families. To the orthodox, the existence of intermediaries between God and people and the possession of spiritual powers are not in accordance with Islamic teachings. The orthodox Muslim regards worship as a direct relationship between people and God. To the Muslim Sudanese, however, whether a Sufi or a non-Sufi, belief in the religious position and powers of the saints in performing miracles constitutes part of his living religion. Because Islam was primarily introduced to the Sudanese by Sufis, the disagreement between the orthodox learned men (ᶜulama) and the Sufis, which is to be found in some Muslim countries, is not a feature of Islam in the Sudan. Indeed, in the Sudan men of religion such as ᶜulama, shaikhs, and fakis(5) are invariably either followers of Sufi orders or in alliance with these orders.

With the introduction of Sufism in the Sudan since the fifteenth century, founders of Sufi orders and their descendants established the Islamic system of education which is still apparent at the present time. In the course of the establishment and spread of the orders, their heads founded Qur'an schools (khalawi; singular: khalwa), and religious lodges, (zawaya; singular: zawiya). These served both as religious schools in which simple arithmetic, Arabic and the Qur'an were taught, and as centres for the followers where they could practise the rituals of the order. With the spread of secular education, the function of the Qur'an school has decreased, though children at pre-elementary schooling age are still to be found there being instructed in the subjects referred to above. The Qur'an school and the lodge are still associated with Sufi orders, and certain functions such as remembrance (dhikr) and the anniversary of the Prophet's birthday (mulid) are sometimes conducted in these institutions. It is not unreasonable to suggest that while the mosque represents orthodox Islam, the Qur'an school and lodge represent Sufism. However, they are all regarded as holy places in which the religious functions of orthodox Islam as well as those of the Sufi orders are performed. Two specifically Sufi practices, the remembrance and the celebration of the anniversary of the Prophet's birthday, are important rituals which the followers are expected to perform. Whenever the mulid is recited the dhikr is repeated. After the recitation of the former, the latter comprises certain repetitions: the name Allah, the formula la ilaha illa 'llah, 'there is no god but Allah', Huwa, 'He', and an attribute of God such as al-Hayy, 'the Living'. The purpose of these repetitions is for a follower to achieve spiritual union with the head of the order and ultimately with God. The mulid was written by the founder of the order and relates the birth, the attributes, the deeds and the death of the Prophet. Fathers always encourage their children to attend this ritual in order to observe and learn, since there is no mode of instruction into the order: rather people 'grow' into it. The mulid is performed on a number of occasions such as naming of the child ceremony, weddings, after recovery from illness, on return from a pilgrimage, on the anniversary of a saint's birth or death (huliyya) and on the Prophet's birthday. Not only is the recitation performed in the rural areas where the orders have influence, but also in the urban centres where each Sufi order performs it in an assigned public place. The ceremony is an occasion celebrated by both Sufi and non-Sufi Muslims.

Sufi orders in the Sudan came to be organized gradually with the purpose of linking the followers in various parts of the country with the spiritual authority. The scale of this organization depended on the size of its following and on the influence of the order. At the apex of the religious hierarchy is the shaikh al-sijjada, leader of the prayer-carpet, who is the spiritual head of the order and whose holiness, which he passes on to his descendants, has been inherited from the founder. Other members of his family are also thought to possess holiness and if the order has a following in various parts of the country, as is the case with the Khatmiyya, for example, they are made responsible for regional centres. The head of the order at any particular time is the ultimate spiritual and temporal authority for his followers. In theory and in practice he is responsible for the welfare of the order and of his followers. For example, he mediates in disputes between followers if these disputes are serious and cannot be solved locally, because the unity of the followers is of significance to the continuity of the order. He intervenes with the authorities on behalf of his followers who seek his help. He nominates and approves condidates for national and local elections. He visits his followers to affirm their allegiance, to deal with affairs brought to his knowledge and to receive

61

their material support. In the past, gifts of land were made to heads of orders, but nowadays economically able followers pay financial contributions. The money collected is used for the upkeep of the family of the head of the order and for the welfare of the order.

Below the head of the order are the khulafa (singular: khalifa), deputies whose title is confirmed upon them by him in view of their devotion, their material assistance and their zeal in spreading the order. They perform a variety of functions: they are the link between the head of the order and the followers, they supervise the performance of rituals in their respective villages or towns, they canvas for the order's candidates in local and national elections, they look after the religious lodges and organize meetings. There are no limits as to the number of appointees to this title which confers prestige and respect. In the case of the Khatmiyya, there exists a title of khalifat al-khulafa, chief deputy, who is chosen from among the deputies, the number of those appointed to this position being very small. They usually supervise the work of deputies and they spend a length of time at the order's headquarters, where they assist the head of the order or are sent on missions to relay instructions on his behalf. The final rung of this hierarchical structure is composed of the followers, who come from different sections of the society and are devoted to the head of the order. The majority of the followers pay allegiance to the order because their forebears did so, and thus belonging to an order has become part of the social tradition of people.

Two further aspects relating to the organization of Sufi orders are of interest. Firstly, orders with a large following, such as the Khatmiyya and Mahdiyya, established headquarters, da'ira, in Khartoum. The headquarters serve as a place for the followers to have audiences with the head of the order, a bureaucratic centre for the order, and a meeting place for the followers. Secondly, the Khatmiyya and Mahdiyya orders found it necessary in the past to establish the Youth Corps (shabab) as a show of strength and to instruct the young in the ways of the order. To distinguish themselves from the rest of the followers, members wear a special and colourful uniform. The ceremonial function of the Youth Corps has gradually decreased with the spread of education.

I have indicated earlier that the politics of the Sudan have been, and still are, influenced by sectarianism. I turn now, therefore, to a discussion of how the orders have come to exercise political influence. The political involvement of Sufi orders began in the nineteenth century during the Turco-Egyptian rule (1821-1885). Sufis were allowed to spread their orders, and gradually heads of orders emerged as respected members of society, who acted as intermediaries between the government and their followers. They were able to act on behalf of the latter in the political field because of the belief that the head of the order acts as representative and master for his followers both in this world and in the world to come(6). Prominent among the orders during this period was the Khatmiyya, whose successive leaders were favoured by the regime. This order was introduced by a non-Sudanese shortly before the Turco-Egyptian conquest of 1820-1821 and gradually acquired support and influence among the tribes of the north and east. The largest tribe in the north, the Shaygiyya, was, and still is, the main supporter of the Khatmiyya. During the Turco-Egyptian period some members of this tribe were employed as army irregulars and tax collectors. Thus it was in the interest of each group - the Government, the Shaygiyya tribe and the Khatmiyya - to support each other in order to maintain their influence and position.

The resentment felt by members of the rival order, the Mahdiyya, towards the favouritism shown to the Khatmiyya order and to the Shaygiyya tribe was a contributory factor in the rise of the Mahdi. The Mahdiyya was, from the beginning, a religious and political movement: the leader of the movement proclaimed himself to be the Mahdi, the 'Expected One' whose message was to establish Islam as a global religion, to bring justice and to dismantle the Turco-Egyptian regime. Althought the Mahdi was a follower of the Sammaniyya order, he requested the heads of the other orders to abandon their paths and join his own mission. Heads of smaller orders joined the Mahdi, but the largest order, the Khatmiyya, did not do so for religious and political reasons. In the rise of the Mahdi, the Khatmiyya saw an end to its privileges, and the head of this order did not acknowledge him as the 'Expected One' since his grandfather had established an order which was the 'seal of all orders' (khatim al-turuq)(7) - hence the name 'Khatmiyya'. Both the Mahdi and the founder of the Khatmiyya order claimed to have revelations from God. The Mahdi succeeded in establishing an Islamic state in 1885, but the Khatmiyya remained in opposition, though its leaders went into voluntary exile in Egypt. The favourable relationship between the Khatmiyya and the Turco-Egyptian ruling authorities laid the foundation for a sympathetic attitude by the Khatmiyya towards Egypt until the present time. Indeed, the Khatmiyya has always advocated the unit of the Nile Valley, i.e. Egypt and Sudan.

With the collapse of the Mahdiyya, which is seen as the first nationalist movement in the Sudan, the Condominium Administration (1898-1956) was established. This was a joint partnership between Egypt and Britain in which the British played the effective role. While the Mahdiyya was suppressed by the authorities, the Khatmiyya, in view of its opposition to the Mahdiyya and its pro-Egyptian stance, was favoured. But the position was later reversed: the Administration helped to re-establish the political force of the Mahdiyya under the posthumous son of al-Mahdi, Sayyid ^{c}Abd al-Rahman, due to the similarity of views over the Sudan's future as an independent nation. The Khatmiyya, on the other hand, fearing the domination of the Mahdiyya, advocated a union between Egypt and Sudan which was not to the liking of the British. Thus, the two orders established themselves as political forces with opposing views involved in the future of the country.

Both orders relied on the rural areas for their principal support, but the small and growing educated class found it necessary to ally themselves either with the Khatmiyya or the Mahdiyya, as they did not have an independent power base in the country at large. Conflicting views as to the political future of the Sudan led to the formation in the 1940's of political parties in which educated people participated. There were two dominant parties: the Umma (the Nation) was formed in 1945 and was composed of Mahdists under the leadership of Sayyid ^{c}Abd al-Rahman, the Ashigga(8) party was formed in 1943 and was composed of Khatmiyya followers in the main together with a non-Khatmiyya group headed by the late President Isma^{c}il al-Azhari, who were supported by Sayyid^{c}Ali al-Mirghani, the head of the Khatmiyya order. The political organization of the Umma and Ashigga parties followed closely that of the religious organization discussed earlier. The majority of adherents to the resulting two political parties were members by virtue of being followers of either the Khatmiyya or the Mahdiyya religious orders. Thus the fusion of religion and politics has been an inseparable aspect of Sudan's politics till the present time.

During the same period, two parties were established which, in theory, were opposed to Sufi orders on ideological and religious grounds: firstly, the Communist Party (1946) which was, and still is, illegal and which drew membership from students, intellectuals, trade unionists and tenant farmers' associations, and secondly, the Muslim Brothers, who also drew their membership from educated people. The political philosophies of these parties filtered to the Sudan from Egypt, and both have established a small but strong following and an effective political organization in the country.

While the Umma remained the Party for the Mahdiyya followers, the Ashigga Party was a combination of Khatmiyya followers and supporters of the late al-Azhari whose aim was also to achieve the unity of the Nile Valley. The alliance between the Khatmiyya and al-Azhari's followers came to be known in 1953 as the National Unionist Party (NUP) instead of the Ashigga. Differences of opinion between the two components of this alliance led to the dismantling of the Party; al-Azhari and his followers retained the name NUP whereas the Khatmiyya established their own party, the

People's Democratic Party (PDP), for the first time in 1956. Thus the two religious orders, the Mahdiyya and Khatmiyya, formed their distinct parties, the Umma and PDP respectively, contesting for power through elections. With Independence in 1956, the struggle between the Mahdiyya and Khatmiyya for political power began, but neither of these orders could form a government in view of their equal strength in parliamentary elections. Khatmiyya influence has been mainly confined to northern and eastern Sudan, whereas that of the Mahdiyya's has been greater in the central and western parts of the country. The party which tipped the balance of power through its alliance in favour of either of the two orders was the NUP, and an understanding was reached whereby the presidency of the Republic was held by a member of this party. Thus alliances between the different political forces became a feature of Sudanese politics during civilian rule. Even the religious differences between the Mahdiyya and Khatmiyya, which are deep-rooted in history and tradition, were on occasions shelved in favour of political alliance. It is said that in sectarian politics favouritism has been shown to its followers, but the followers who are the beneficiaries of this favouritism see it as a consequence of the mutual interest and dependence between them and the religious orders.

The politics of alliance were interrupted by the first military takeover in 1958 which resulted in a dissolution of the Constitutional Assembly and a ban on all political parties. However, the power of the opposition comprising various political forces both religious and secular, resulted in the army handing over power to the civilians in 1964 as a result of peaceful civilian demonstrations. The politics of alliance returned to the political scene with the dominance, as before, of both the Khatmiyya and the Mahdiyya. During this period, which lasted from 1964 till 1969, the Umma Party saw a rift within its leadership which both weakened its position and resulted in the creation of two factions. In contrast, the old alliance between the Khatmiyya (PDP) and al-Azhari's followers (NUP) was revived and both groups formed a new party under the name of Democratic Unionist Party (DUP) in 1967. A national election was held in 1968 in which the DUP and a faction of the Umma under the leadership of the late religious leader of the Mahdiyya, al-Hadi al-Mahdi, formed an alliance, but the outstanding problem as to who should be the future president of the Republic remained unresolved. The alliance was unable to resolve this problem when the army took power for the second time in May 1969. As under the first military takeover, the Constitutional Assembly was dissolved and political parties were banned.

Since 1969 until the present-time, the regime has encountered political instability and economic difficulties. Among several unsuccessful coups, two are of significance:

the first by the army in 1972 with the support of the communists and the second in 1976 involving an armed invasion of the capital organized primarily by the Mahdists with Libyan support. In both these significant attempts many people were killed, executed or imprisoned. The present regime's continually changing alliances with certain internal political groups and with other foreign countries have added to the state of instability and uncertainty in its policies. This is further reflected in endemic ministerial reshuffles and cyclical changes in personnel. The regime, by its military nature, is authoritarian, and real power is in the hands of the President. Moreover, in place of the former multi-party democracy, the regime has introduced a one-party system, the Sudan Socialist Union (SSU). This party in theory is intended to include all shades of political views; in practice it encompasses people who must support the regime, while opposition to the political authority is not tolerated within it. In spite of the support given to the SSU both in the south and north of Sudan, many supporters in the north have continued their allegiance to the traditional political parties. The SSU relies in part for its support on people in government service for whom party membership is obligatory. Other people not in the same category are free to make their own decisions or membership. While there are many who advocate a policy of non-co-operation with the SSU, others who are members seek to dominate the SSU in order to sway its policies in the interests of their traditional political and religious associations. There is a consensus among Sudanese that their political and religious affiliations are deep rooted and that a centrally imposed party is in contradiction to the democratic tradition to which they have been accustomed. People seek to preserve their political and religious identity and want to be allowed to express their views freely.

The recognition of the existence of different political forces was acknowledged by the present regime through the National Reconciliation of 1977. The regime recognized the role and strength of the various political parties, but not all of them were allowed, or even willing, to participate in this reconciliation. The only political group which is presently in alliance with the regime is the organization of the Muslim Brothers, but its inclusion is not because of a meeting of 'minds' so much as for political expediency. The two religious orders, the Mahdiyya and Khatmiyya, are politically out of favour. While the Mahdiyya has taken active and sometimes armed opposition against the regime, the Khatmiyya has adopted a cautious stance in the belief that it cannot risk an armed uprising to take over power, something which it has never attempted in the past. Even to contemplate such a policy would be unacceptable to the Khatmiyya leaders and followers.

Economically, the country is in acute financial

difficulties: there is a very large international debt, high inflation, lack of foreign exchange, chronic shortages of basic commodities and spare parts, declining agricultural and industrial output, mismanagement, corruption, huge investment in prestigious development projects, and an exodus of much-needed qualified personnel, mainly to the Arab oil-producing countries. This has resulted in a severe strain on the economic resources of the country and justifiable concern. Recent strikes and protests reflect people's disapproval of and lack of confidence in the policies of the present regime.

With the aforementioned political and economic difficulties in mind, Sudanese pose the problem: what alternatives are there should the regime collapse? The answer is complex, reflecting the diversity of political views. However, there is a consensus that different political parties should be allowed to operate freely, contrary to the practice nowadays. Thus, despite their shortcomings, there is nostalgia for past periods of civilian rule during which there was freedom of expression for individuals and political parties. Civilian rule through multi-party democracy has not been given sufficient time to prove its viability. Indeed, in the twenty-six years since Sudan's independence, twenty years have been dominated by military rule.

Despite the endeavours by military regimes to exclude the religious orders from participation in politics, both the Mahdiyya and Khatmiyya have continued to hold political ambitions, whether in or out of government, in view of the support still rendered to them. Even if they are banned politically, they cannot be stopped from existing and operating as religious orders, and when the time is ripe they can reaffirm among their followers a political loyalty which is fundamentally a religious one. The strength of these orders should not be underrated, in that they play a significant role in the religious life of the Sudanese. Islam in the Sudan has many channels: the official religion, the religious orders, and the beliefs and practices associated with them which have come to be incorporated in Islam, these latter being part of the people's life and social systems.

Critics of the participation by religious orders in politics have been the army, the educated people and the Muslim Brothers. The army has always advocated the secularity of politics, and has excluded both sectarian and secular parties unless they participate on the army's terms. The two successful army coups of 1958 and 1969 were staged in the belief that traditional party politics, which include sectarianism, are conservative and detrimental to progress. Apart from the army, another group who neither adhere to nor tolerate the religious orders are some educated people who advocate that these latter should confine themselves to the field of religion and leave politics to the literate and educated people. Their stance is based on the assumption that the support enjoyed by religious orders is composed of illiterate people who have blind obedience to the heads of orders and who lack political awareness or understanding. From the point of view of the followers, just as they respect the religious authority of the head of the order so also should they adhere to his political stand because of their belief that he knows better and his authority cannot be questioned. In practice, the followers respect the decisions and recommendations of the head of the order because they believe that he has their interests and welfare at heart. Educated people think that, with the spread of education and the secularization of politics, the influence of religious orders will disappear - a point of view which is debatable. People who cannot read and write do not lack political awareness or maturity. Sectarianism and sectarian politics have deep-rooted convictions which have been adhered to by people over generations. While the head of an order has the final say in making decisions, there has always existed a dialogue, channelled through his representatives, between him and his followers. Unlike the vacillating political stands of the educated people, followers of a particular religious order are committed to its politics. Disenchantment with a secular political structure and authority strengthens further people's resolve to use Islam as a unifying factor and a movement of protest. The role of religion in politics is not peculiar to the Sudan, as is demonstrated by recent events in Egypt, Syria and Iran.

In the Sudan, while the army has power, the educated people are powerless unless they are in alliance either with the traditional parties, as happened in the past, or, since 1969, with the army. Unlike the religious orders, educated people do not possess a power base and their influence is confined to urban centres. The rural areas encompass about three-quarters of the total population and it is in these areas that the influence of religious orders is prominent. Educated people have a useful role to play in the development of the country, but it is unrealistic on their part to assume that they have a better understanding of politics than people who lack formal education. The present alliance between the educated people and the army has not given a positive political lead to convince the so-called illiterate people that their traditional political association with religious orders is no longer viable.

With the exception of the Muslim Brothers, the established clergy have not pronounced public criticism of the beliefs and practices of religious orders, since it is felt this could lead to religious strife. In contrast, the Muslim Brothers, who advocate the establishment of an Islamic state with Islam as the basis of legislation, reject the concept of union with God, since it was not preached during the early period of Islam. Moreover, they point out that the position and title of the head of the order, <u>sidi</u>, master, is inconsistent with the concept of God in Islam. To the fundamentalists, God is the only Master, not the head of the order, whose powers of intercession between God and the followers are disclaimed by them. Critics of the Muslim Brothers point out that the establishment of an Islamic state will be unacceptable to the non-Muslim people of the country and that any government attempting to achieve this will be faced with political difficulties. Sufism and the belief in the power of the saints are an integral parts of the religion of the Sudanese which has developed in its present day form since the fifteenth century. Thus Sufi religious orders have a strong and real claim to represent Islam in the country.

The other extremist political group is the communists. Unlike the followers of religious orders and the Muslim Brothers, this party advocates the secularity of politics, and from its ideological standpoint there is no part for religion to play in politics. However, both the Muslim Brothers and the communists who represent opposing ideologies tend to overlook the reality of the religious, social and political associations of people in the society. Their respective ideologies, particularly that of the Communists, will not be acceptable to the majority of the rural population among whom the orders have influence.

Critics of religious orders tend to underestimate the reasons for their influence and continuity. In politics, the religious orders do not advocate an extremist ideology as do the communists and the Muslim Brothers, whose political views are not acceptable to the Sudanese nation as a whole. Through past experience, religious orders have found it necessary to establish alliances and by so doing they have recognized the necessity for political co-operation as well as for the independence of political groupings. The need for political alliances in Sudanese politics points to the fact that no single party is dominant and able to rule on its own. Therefore, if political stability is to be achieved then all political forces should be given the right of participation in the political field. The experience of governing the country without the participation of the various political forces, particularly the two major religious orders, has proved to be uneasy. Nevertheless, the present regime has survived since 1969, despite facing difficulties, a fact which is attributed to military support.

The theme of this paper has been the role of the religious orders in the religion and politics of the Sudan. Do they have a place and a role in modern Sudan? The answer lies in the factors which have contributed to the continuity of their role in society. The beliefs and practices of the religious orders are part of people's beliefs in Islam. These beliefs are not abandoned with political change because they form part of the ideology and value system handed down to the followers of religious orders from previous generations. Leaders of such orders are respected members of society in view of their religious position and political role. They are heads of religious and political organizations which draw their main support from the rural areas where their strength lies. Religious orders have created religious and political ties cross-cutting tribal, territorial and occupational affiliations. The Sudanese, like many other nations in the world, have a multiple identity. The ethnic, religious, cultural and political complexity of the country has given rise to social diversity, and in this context traditional loyalties and personal identification with a country, a tribe, a place, a language, a religion, and a religious order is essential to the individual. These loyalties are strong among peoples in the rural areas of the Sudan and they also operate in the heterogeneous urban centres where an individual relies upon his loyalties for security, access to employment and personal assurance. Thus the national unity of the Sudanese is dependent on the recognition and acceptance of the ethnic, political, religious and cultural diversity which makes the Sudan such a complex and interesting country.

NOTES

1. My thanks to the Ford Foundation and the Nuffield Foundation for their grants towards my anthropological fieldwork among the Shaygiyya tribe of northern Sudan. My thanks also to my wife, Anne, for her valuable comments.
2. Wad Dayf Allah, Muhammad, Kitab al-tabaqat, in Arabic (Cairo, 1930). The book contains biographies of men of religion who helped in spreading Islam and Sufi orders during the Funji Kingdom of Sennar (16th century - 19th century). The biographies have been translated into English: MacMichael, Sir Harold A., A History of the Arabs in the Sudan, vol. 2 (London, 1967), pp.217-272.
3. turuq (singular: tariqa or tawa'if (singular: ta'ifa). Throughout this paper, both these terms are translated as orders.
4. A later development in Sufism is the doctrine of al-nur al-Muhammadiyya, 'the light of Muhammad', which is the first thing God created and of which the world is a manifestation. In the Sudan for example, the mulid, an allegorical life of Prophet Muhammad, of the Khatmiyya Sufi order, written by its founder, clearly states the creation and significance of this doctrine. See Al-Mirghani, Sayyid Muhammad ^cUthman, Mawlid al-Nabi, in Arabic (Egypt, 1932), pp.6-10.
5. ^culama (singular: ^calim), religious scholars. Shaikh is a title to denote the head of a Sufi order, a man of

religion not necessarily a Sufi, or a village headman. Faki (a corruption of faqih) is a teacher in a Qur'an school who also plays the role of a healer.
6. This duality is well stated in the following oath of allegiance recited by a person on joining the Khatmiyya order:

In the name of the Merciful and Compassionate God. O God I have repented before you and have agreed that my master, sidi, Muhammad ᶜUthman will be my shaikh in this world and the one to come. O God make firm my love towards him. Amen

7. The founder studied the paths of the following Sufi orders: Naqshabandiyya, Qadiriyya, Shadhiliyya, Junaidiyya and Mirghaniyya (which was founded by his father). He adopted the formula of NAQSHJAM as the symbol of the spiritual chain represented by these orders.
8. Ashigga is an Arabic word (ashiqqa') denoting brothers by the same father and mother.

REFERENCES

Bechtold, P.K. (1976) Politics in the Sudan: Parliamentary and Miilitary Rule in an Emerging African Nation, New York
Holt, P.M. and Daly, M.W. (1979) The History of the Sudan, London
MacMichael, Sir Harold A. (1967) A History of the Arabs in the Sudan, 2nd impression, 2 vols., London
Mohamed Omer Beshir (1974) Revolution and Nationalism in the Sudan, London
Muddathir Abd al-Rahim (1969) Imperialism and Nationalism in the Sudan, Oxford
Al-Shahi, Ahmed (1969) 'Politics and the Role of Women in a Shaiqiya Constituency - 1968', Sudan Society, 4, pp.27-38
Idem., (1979) 'Traditional Politics and A One Party System in Northern Sudan', Bulletin of the British Society for Middle Eastern Studies, 6, 1, pp.3-12
Idem., (1981) 'Noah's Ark: The Continuity of the Khatmiyya Order in Northern Sudan', Bulletin of the British Society for Middle Eastern Studies, 8, 1, pp.13-29
Trimingham, J.S. (1965) Islam in the Sudan, 2nd impression, London
Voll, J.O. (1978) A History of the Khatmiyyah Tariqah in the Sudan, University Micro-Films International, Ann Arbor, Michigan
Warburg, G. (1978) Islam, Nationalism and Communism in a Traditional Society: The Case of Sudan, London
Willis, C.A. (1921) 'Religions Confraternities of the Sudan',

Sudan Notes and Records, 4, 4, pp.175-194

BEKTASHIS IN TURKEY

J.D. Norton

Historically, the Bektashi(1) Order was, by common consent, one of the most important Sufi orders, (tarikats)(2) in the Ottoman Empire. It has survived repeated attempts to destroy it and, although officially proscribed, it still commands the devotion of thousands, possibly millions, of followers. The aims of this paper are to outline developments in the order particularly since the foundation of the Turkish Republic in 1923, and to note the nature of Bektashi activity and allegiance today.

English readers will find Bektashi history, beliefs and practices, as they were in Ottoman times, recorded in some detail by Hasluck(3) and Birge(4), but little is generally known of the present situation.

The Bektashi order is a Shi^{c}i, Ja^{c}fari, mainly Turkish tarikat. Bektashis believe their founder, Hajji Bektash, was born in Khurasan in the thirteenth century A.D. and, imbued with the teachings of Ahmet Yesevi (Ahmad al-Yasawi), came to Anatolia and established his headquarters in the place that today bears his name, Hacıbektaş, which lies between Kırşehir and Nevşehir, some 150 miles from Ankara. From here he is said to have striven to raise Turkish morale and consolidate Islam in Asia Minor at that time of great upheavals when Muslims and Christians alike were seeking to prove by force of arms the superiority of their own faith, and when rival peoples were contesting possession of the land. A popular, but erroneous tradition links Hajji Bektash with the founding of the Janissaries, the corps d'elite of the Ottoman army at the time of its greatest triumphs, but a body that later degenerated into a rebellious rabble powerful enough to overthrow sultans but no longer capable of protecting the Empire. In fact, the longstanding connection between the Janissaries and the Bektashis began years after the death of Hajji Bektash. It was a connection that contributed considerably to the spread of the sect throughout the Ottoman Empire. Bektashism grew strong in the Balkans, especially Albania, as well as in Anatolia, and later Bektashis boasted

73

Bektashis in Turkey

that a traveller would find a Bektashi tekke(5) (Ar. takiyya) no more than six hours journey (15 miles) apart throughout the Empire(6). Syncretism and heterodoxy have always been marked features of Bektashism. Several pre-Islamic Turkish customs from Central Asia were continued and a number of new heresies began to take root in the movement, but in about 1500 Balim Sultan, the figure regarded as the Order's second founder, made vigorous efforts to halt the degeneration of the sect. He is credited with introducing some order into the Order. He institued a Bektashi hierarchy and established a successful form of organization as well as purging at least some of the wide variety of unorthodox beliefs.

Bektashis often refer to four grades introduced by Balim Sultan(7). These are:

Aşık (Ar. ^cashiq) or kalender: those seeking full admission to the Order and undergoing instruction for initiation.

Dervish: those who had been accepted into the Order.

Baba: those who, after a period of service and study in the grade of Dervish, are elected to lead and instruct groups of Dervishes and aşıks.

Dedebaba: the baba elected to head the whole movement. Until the dissolution of the tarikats in 1925 he was based at Hacıbektas at the tekke where the founding saint lies buried.

Between baba and dedebaba there is what amounts to an additional grade of halife (Ar. khalifa). A halife is a baba appointed by the dedebaba to exercise authority in a specific area, an arrangement analagous to that between archbishops and bishops. Some Bektashis add more grades and make finer distinctions between them, but more important is the fact that a very large number of those who consider themselves Bektashis do not accept the concept of elected leaders, particularly elected dedebabas. This arises from the longstanding division between the 'Yol Evladı' and the 'Bel Evladı'. The Yol Evladı (Children of the Way) believe that Hajji Bektash did not marry and had no children. They hold that true membership of the Order is gained by initiation at a special ceremony (Ayin-i Cem), following a period of instruction from a mürşit (Ar. murshid, spiritual guide). Their babas elect as dedebaba the person they deem most worthy of that office. Within this main division of Bektashism there are some who hold that celibacy should be a precondition of high office, but these are in a dwindling minority. The Bel Evladı (natural descendants) claim that

74

Hajji Bektash did marry and had a son and that Bektashi leadership rightfully belongs to his physical descendants. These were known as Çelebis, and many village groups accepted their spiritual authority. Since such groups are themselves descended from the early followers of Hajji Bektash, membership of them, like nationality, is conferred by birth, and no special initiation ceremony is required(8). The dedebabas of both these kinds of Bektashis were based at Hacibektas and both of them received tribute from their widespread groups of followers.

This situation complicates the problem of how to define a Bektashi and how to assess their numbers. Some claim that within Turkey there is no distinction between Alevi and Bektashi(9), but this is an exaggeration. Though all Turkish Alevis and Türkmen (Tahtacıs) revere Hajji Bektash, some would acknowledge a prior allegiance to other saints and would not claim to be Bektashis(10). The numerical strength of the tarikat is now impossible to gauge with accuracy. The Turkish quinquennial census records religion but not tarikat (it could scarcely do so, since the Orders are illegal). The estimates given by members often seem, in the absence of supporting evidence, to be more optimistic than reliable. Claims that there are about fourteen million or more are frequently heard. Today there are still both Yol Evladı (who tend to refer to themselves simply as 'Bektashis') and Bel Evladı (who often call themselves and refer to their sect as 'Alevi-Bektashi'). Both sorts are scattered throughout many parts of Turkey, the areas where they are particularly strong including Tokat, Sivas, Central Anatolia, Denizli and Izmir. Yol Evladı possibly have more town dwellers than peasants in their ranks, and Bel Evladı a higher proportion of villagers. Istanbul, Ankara and Izmir have flourishing groups, and research has shown that some peasants moving to the towns in the course of Turkey's rapid urbanisation rekindle an interest in Bektashism which they may have allowed to lapse at home. In their new surroundings, these people find Bektashism offers a comforting reminder of home and provides a mutual support system.

Being a Shi'i sect in a Sunni state always posed problems for the Bektashis; their relations with the authorities were at best uneasy, often rebellious. Doubts about their political loyalty plus their disregard for standard Islamic observances, while at the same time indulging in heretical practices, often led to their being persecuted. Persecution strengthened their inclination to conduct their affairs in secret. The resultant aura of mystery this produced attracted some new members but also provided ammunition for their opponents who accused them of licentiousness because men and unveiled women took part as equals in Bektashi ceremonies, and, to make matters worse, alcohol was drunk and the proceedings were often enlivened by music and dancing!

Certainly the Bektashis have never attached much importance to the formal requirements of Islam. The 'five pillars' count for little. To the standard declaration of faith a further line is added to include reference to ^{c}Ali(11). Indeed, it is often claimed that Bektashis see Allah, Muhammad and ^{c}Ali as forming a trinity(12). Bektashis frequently assert that Muhammad and ^{c}Ali are one and indistinguishable(13), though in practice the chief focus of their love is ^{c}Ali. Very few Bektashis perform the ritual act of prayer, namaz, or attend mosques – which they often regard as places where hatred of ^{c}Ali and his followers is propagated. Hardly any Bektashis fast during Ramadan, though a form of fast is observed in the first twelve days of the month Muharram and the three preceding days of Dhu 'l-Hijja. The obligation to give alms, they believe, is subsumed in the Bektashi obligation to help all who are in need and the Bektashi tradition of mutual support. Bektashis do not make the pilgrimage to Mecca. (One often hears them lamenting the drain on Turkey's currency reserves caused by the thousands of Sunni pilgrims going to Saudi Arabia.) For Bektashis the main place of pilgrimage is Hacıbektaş, though there are numerous other shrines that the devout take pleasure in visiting, too.

Before the ban on tarikats, Bektashi gatherings were usually held in tekkes or other suitable buildings, including private homes. It was customary for outsiders to be excluded and a veil of secrecy to be drawn over the proceedings – similar to a Freemasons' gathering. The assembled initiates would recite and sing verses that form part of the rich heritage of Bektashi literature. (These were usually in pure Turkish, such as would appeal to the common man. Consequently, Bektashi literature has retained its appeal, whereas that of the other tarikats that made greater use of Arabic, Ottoman or Persian elements is largely incomprehensible in Republican Turkey since Atatürk's language purification measures have taken effect.) Music would usually accompany the hymn-singing, and special dances of symbolic significance would further assist the attainment of a state of spiritual ecstasy. All this continues today. At certain meetings, sins are confessed, disputes adjudicated and punishments awarded. Eating and drinking and conversation have always been important elements of many Bektashi gatherings, the basis of the meal usually being a sacrificed sheep. Wine and/or raki (Ar. ^{c}araq) are distributed by the saki (wine bearers). During the conversation, known as sohbet, Bektashi beliefs, traditions and opinions are reiterated and the babas answer questions from their flocks and give further teachings.

These teachings are designed to lead the follower through the four states of enlightenment known as the four gateways: Sheriat (Ar. shari^{c}a), Tarikat (Ar. tariqa),

Marifet (Ar. ma^{c}rifa), and Hakikat (Ar. haqiqa). These four stages are explained in different ways by different Bektashis. Many liken them to a process of growth from seed to flower to unripe nut and finally to mature nut. The first gateway, Sheriat, is orthodox Islamic teaching. (In practice Bektashis do not linger long in this gateway!) Tarikat, the second gateway, is the teaching and practices of the secret Order itself. Marifet is the gateway to mystic knowledge of God, and Hakikat is the immediate experience of the essence of Reality.

Underlying much Bektashi teaching is the concept of the unity of existence (vahdet-i vücut, Ar. wahdat al-wujud) the positive expression of which prompts them to seek God within themselves(14) and to love all creation as different manifestations of the One Being. The emphasis in their teaching is upon love, friendship, truth, tolerance and sincerity, and avoidance of what they condemn as the narrow, bigoted hypocrisy of those who, like the scribes and Pharisees of the New Testament, observe the letter but deny the spirit of the Law. Their own moral code they hold to be much superior to that of the orthodox Sunnis. Bektashis simply counsel self-control to avoid harming others by word or deed, summarising this in Turkish as: 'Eline, diline, beline sahip ol'. They have always acknowledged that women have rights equal to those of men. They attach great importance to education. They value artistic expression: representations of some of their revered figures are among the most prized possessions safeguarded in their tekkes(15).

A great deal has been written about 'the Bektashi secret' - most of it contradictory. The mystery has intrigued the curious and given opportunities for detractors to calumniate the Order. There are teachings reserved for the initiated, who, like Freemasons, are forbidden to reveal them to outsiders. The wide variety of 'secrets' that have been said to be THE SECRET range from doctrinal revelations and cosmological teachings to glimpses of treasured pictures(16).

It is not surprising that so many different versions of 'the Bektashi secret' should be confidently asserted: Bektashis pride themselves on being undogmatic and tolerant, so beneath the broad umbrella of Bektashism some groups teach ideas that others reject, and even some of the most commonly held basic teachings can be difficult to reconcile with one another. To cite but one example, the concept of unity of existence and the consequent obligation to love all creation would appear to conflict with teberra (Ar. tabarra), the requirement to withhold love from or even to hate those who do not revere ^{c}Ali and his family, the 'Ehl-i beyt' (Ar. ahl al-bait)(17). Hasluck aptly summarized the situation as follows:

> The religious doctrines of the Bektashi are devised to cater for all intellects and all temperaments: their system

includes, like other mystic religions, a gradual initiation to secret knowledge by a number of grades: these form a series of steps between crude and popular religion, in which saintworship plays an important part, to a very emancipated, in some respects enlightened, philosophy. The theology of Bektashism ranges from pantheism to atheism(18).

Bektashi rejection of orthodoxy had always attracted many political dissidents to its ranks, and this further increased the antipathy of the authorities and led to frequent persecutions, sometimes borne with great fortitude. Often Bektashis had to rely upon wit to deflect the wrath of their rulers, and this reflected in countless Bektashi jokes that remain popular in Turkey to this day. Suffering at the hands of the authorities was, of course, a reality of life for many Shi^cis beyond the bounds of the Ottoman Empire, too. The observation made by Gustav Thaiss very often applied to the suffering of the Bektashis:

> ...basic to the Shi^ca world view is a sense of persecution - unjust persecution. Much as the underlying assumptions of Freudian psychoanalysis focus on certain negative attributes of the personality, so the Shi^ca are preconditioned to see the negative, the sad, the tragic and those who are persecuted. The Shi^ca see themselves in a passive situation as people who are and have been acted upon(19).

But at times the Bektashis attempted to rebel, and their literature praises the stand against tyranny made by such heroes as the sixteenth century Pir Sultan Abdal, who, according to tradition, was hanged for his part in a rebellion(20).

The Bektashi association with the Janissaries led to a determined attempt to wipe out the Order when the Janissaries were destroyed by Mahmud II in 1826. Leading Bektashis were executed or exiled. A number of Bektashi properties were razed, other handed over to the Nakshibendi (Naqshabandi) Order. Birge(21) reports a popular story that Mahmud II vowed to execute 70,000 Bektashis and when he could not find that many to behead he ordered headpieces to be cut off Bektashi tombstones to make up the number!

The longstanding Bektashi practice of conducting their affairs in secret no doubt helped the Order to survive this savage setback, and by the middle of the nineteenth century they were again strong. According to Şapolyo(22), Sultan ^cAbd al-^cAziz, who reigned from 1861 to 1876, was himself a Bektashi. Birge(23) mentions a belief that this sultan's mother was one. In the reign of ^cAbd al-Hamid II (1876-1909) the Bektashi Order proved useful to the Young Turks, who found its network of tekkes, its penchant for secrecy, and its predisposition to oppose the central government valuable assets in their fight against the sultan's tyranny. During the First World War, the Çelebi Bektashi leader raised a volunteer regiment and took it to fight on the eastern front against the Russians. In the subsequent War of Independence, he and his younger brother, who succeeded him in 1921, declared their support for Mustafa Kemal and, it is said, were among the first to learn of his plans to declare a Republic(24). This support did not prevent the Bektashis, along with all other tarikats, from being proscribed in 1925 under Law No. 677(25). All Bektashi tekkes were closed and their property seized. Some of the contents of the tekke at Hacıbektaş were removed to museums - mostly to the Ethnographic Museum in Ankara - to be exhibited as relics of a bygone age. The purpose of banning the tarikats was twofold: to destroy possible centres of disaffection and revolt and to replace the reactionary influence of mürşits, who taught arcane mysteries, by the influence of modern teachers who were to imbue Turkish people with Ataturk's vision of a new, westward-looking nation. The message is still emblazoned across the front of Ankara University:'"Hayatta en hakiki mürşit ilimdir". Atatürk' (The truest guide in life is Science).

Naturally, this crippling blow was a severe disappointment to the Bektashis, many of whom had nourished hopes that Bektashism would be made the official religion of the state. Nevertheless, they tried to make the best of the inevitable and, publicly at least, to console themselves with the claim that the Republic had brought about many of the things which Bektashis had supported and preserved for centuries, for example, greater freedom for women than was normal in orthodox Islam. Fortunately the intentions of some extreme secularists to blow up the tekke and other sacred sites at Hacıbektaş were not implemented. Some influential people recognised that Bektashis had indeed several points in common with the new ideals Atatürk was striving to realise. In matters of language they had always sought to convey their message in the language of whatever area they were in. Thus, in Turkey the Kemalists could not but approve the Bektashi preference for Turkish of the pure as opposed to the Ottoman variety. Bektashis' liberal ideas and their liking for alcohol were further plus factors as far as Turkey's new rulers were concerned. But the ban on tarikats was strictly enforced, so the Bektashi Order once more went deeply underground and stayed there for nearly four decades.

When it gradually re-emerged, its new look bore interesting features. The introduction of party politics in Turkey after World War Two led to a relaxation of the anti-religious drive, and when Menderes was in power in the 1950s, restoration work began on the tekke building at Hacıbektaş. This was continued after the 1960 coup d'etat,

and the tekke was opened - as a museum - on 16th August
1964, after a closure of almost 39 years. From that time on,
annual Bektashi celebrations have been held at Hacıbektaş in
mid-August, providing a good opportunity to observe certain
developments(26), including the way in which Bektashis have
endeavoured to make themselves acceptable to the authorities
and general public, the revival of ancient traditions, the
survival of normal tarikat activities in secret, and the
intrustion of politics.

The existence of the Festival illustrates the Turkish flair
for getting round inconvenient legislation. Since in Turkey
tarikats were banned but tourism was encouraged, the festival
was promoted as a tourist attraction. Since 1953 the Mevlevis
had been allowed an annual whirl in public in Konya for the
benefit of visitors, so the Bektashis followed this example and
put on their three-day celebrations as a tourist festival
honouring Hajji Bektash, who was portrayed as a great
Turkish philosopher.

The emphasis on Turkishness became strident and
insistent. This is in sharp contrast to Hasluck's observation
early in the present century: '...the Bektashi sect is
identified with no nation or race'(27). Now, Turkish
Bektashis take every opportunity to put forward Hajji Bektash
as a sort of patron saint of Turkey. This, of course, is
popular with Turkish audiences and, Bektashis hope, will
make the authorities reluctant to clamp down on their
activities. So, Hajji Bektash is portrayed as having been sent
from Khurasan with a divine message specifically for Turks, a
Turkish pioneer in Anatolia, a Turkish liberator. Placed at
the top of one list of his sayings is the statement: 'The
Turkish nation was created to rule the world'(28). Articles in
the national press around festival time take a similar line,
emphasising the Turkishness of the Order, its assocation with
the Janissaries and its contributions to pure Turkish language
and literature.

The Turkish emphasis is seen in the religious
interpretations of some Bektashis, too. It is not unusual for
them to regard both Muhammad and ^{c}Ali as Turks. Just as
some sincere, simple English Christians might picture Jesus as
an Anglo-Saxon, so, when the festival audience at Hacibektas
sings hymns of praise to ^{c}Ali, they think in terms of a
Turkish ^{c}Ali(29). Some prominent Bektashis take this even
further and claim explicitly and publicly that Muhammad and
^{c}Ali were Turks(30).

The strong Turkish emphasis is one element in
present-day Bektashism shared both by what might be termed
the 'religious Bektashis' and by the 'political Bektashis'.
'Religious Bektashis' are here taken to mean those whose
prime concern is with the sincere veneration of ^{c}Ali in the
traditional Bektashi manner, including the continuation of
Bektashi religious teachings and customs, whereas 'political

Bektashis' are those who have no interest in such matters as the racial origins of the Prophet but see the chief value of Bektashism as being a movement that could help to bring about a more just society organized in accordance with socialist principles. Although the exploitation of religion for political purposes was forbidden by the Constitution, the Right had for a long time been exploiting Sunni sentiment. In the 1960s their opponents responded by seeking Bektashi and Alevi votes. The Birlik Partisi (Unity Party), founded in 1966, actually used the lion and twelve stars (symbolising ᶜAli and the Twelve Imams) as its party emblem. But this party did not make effective use of the Bektashi network, and its supporters felt betrayed when it backed Demirel in a crucial vote. The mildly left-of-centre Republican People's Party, as well as more extreme left-wing organisations, made vigorous efforts to gain the support of the Bektashis, since they could prove valuable carriers of a political message across the land.

By the mid-1970s the results of their efforts were visible in the changed nature of the annual festival. The original, cautious organizing committee, mostly 'religious Bektashis' steeped in Bektashi legends and devoted to the teachings of the tarikat, had been voted out by young men impatient for social change and calling for political activism. They dropped the Janissary bands that had been a feature of the earlier festivals and in their place invited left-wing writers, singers and composers to slant the proceedings towards politics and away from religion and tourism. Their emphasis on the Turkishness of the movement was intended to demonstrate that Hajji Bektash had preached resistance to foreign influences. Fortunately for all concerned, the details of Hajji Bektash's life are conveniently vague, so confident assertions of his views can be made without fear of refutation. Thus he was portrayed as one who opposed the 'corrupting' Persian and Arab ideas that the Seljuk rulers in 13th century Anatolia had adopted. The parallel was drawn with Anatolia of the 1970s. Hajji Bektash was revealed as the opponent of Western capitalism and of American imperialist ambitions in Turkey. He was shown on posters as a champion in the fight against fascism. He was said to point the way to socialism. 'Hajji Bektash', they declared, 'was not, as many people think a religious leader, a saint or a seer, he was a socialist revolutionary thinker and leader who...brought a plan for a new, human social system'(31).

Every opportunity was taken to drive home this message. It was expressed with varying degrees of circumspection at the opening ceremonies and repeated and discussed at length at the lectures and seminars that have been a feature of the festival since 1975. Prominent left-wing authors, with or without Bektashi connections, were invited to address meetings, and well-known ozan (wandering minstrels) put over the same message to music to the thousands who attended the open-air entertainment after dark. (These ozan are often said to be among the most potent influences upon public opinion in rural Turkey.) Several, but by no means all, of the ozan who came to Hacıbektaş openly professed Marxism and others were considerably further to the Left. There were usually many people in the audience who wanted to hear their undiluted message, even at the risk of incurring the wrath of the authorities. In the late 1970s, for example, there were vociferous demands for 'Kızıldere', a song eulogising the young men who were killed after kidnapping foreign NATO technicians near the Black Sea coast a few years earlier.

It began to seem that Bektashis, for centuries conditioned to see themselves as victims of oppression and injustice, were no longer content to be merely observers of the political scene. Some of them, particularly the younger ones, saw Bektashism not as a way to make loss and wordly defeat endurable but as a means of securing change. They interpreted the tragedy of Pir Sultan Abdal not as an object lesson in how to resign oneself to death with dignity but as a clarion call to wholehearted opposition to tyranny. Their fervour and single-mindedness were sometimes couterproductive and frequently brought them into conflict with 'religious Bektashis' and older people and several local communities as well as with the authorities.

Government attitudes towards the Bektashis are plainly reflected in the treatment of the annual festival. In 1977, with a right-wing government in power, the festival committee complained that their plans had been frustrated. Performance of the play 'Pir Sultan Abdal' was banned. Alterations were made to the rest of the programme. Some ozan were not allowed. Some speakers felt it unwise to be forthright in expressing their political views. Most noticeable of all was the massive military presence, which was doubly objectionable since it not only cast an oppressive shadow over the proceedings but also deprived visitors of facilities for eating and sleeping, because the school buildings previously made available for them were used as accommodation for the troops. In 1978, under a left-of-centre government, the situation was entirely different. Only as many extra police as were thought necessary to control the additional traffic were drafted in. The performance of 'Pir Sultan Abdal' was allowed. No restrictions were placed on the choice of ozan or what they chose to sing. The Prime Minister, Bülent Ecevit, himself was expected to come and lay the foundation stone of a covered sports hall. In the event, he was unable to attend but he sent no less that three of his ministers, who vied with one another in the promises they made to the people of Hacıbektaş. Needless to say, they were rapturously received. But still there were many voices preaching the need for faster, more radical change. The politicization of the movement and of the annual celebrations deeply offended and saddened most of the 'religious Bektashis'. Some of the older ones suffered an added disappointment because they did not receive from revolutionary youth the respect that age used to command. The religious Bektashis carefully avoided involvement in politics and used their visit to Hacıbektaş as an opportunity to pay their respects to important babas, meet in private to sacrifice and feast and talk together about their beliefs and traditions and, in many cases, to practise those traditions by doing the rounds of pilgrimage at Hacıbektaş.

A typical round would include visits to several revered sites in and around the tiny town (population around 6,000) of Hacıbektaş. These include the tekke, the 'horse-rock', the 'vineyard', the 'five stones', Kadıncık Evi, Mount Arafat, Zemzem Fountain, and Çilehane. The crowds going to these sites include both devout Bektashis and ordinary festival visitors in holiday mood. There is no fixed order in which the sites have to be visited and not every devotee goes to every site - some are several kilometres away along dusty tracks.

Almost everyone goes to the tekke complex. Visitors there might drink from the lion fountain in the second courtyard before passing through the third gateway and thence to the main building that contains the tombs of Hajji Bektash and several of his leading followers. They will see the Kırklar Meydanı - the main hall in which the most important ceremonies used to be performed. Within the same inner courtyard stands the mausoleum of Balım Sultan, outside which is an aged mulberry tree festooned with strips of material, all tied on by people praying that a loved one's sickness may be cured.

After leaving the tekke, the 'horse-rock' may be visited. Hajji Bektash is said to have demonstrated miraculous power upon this rock when a rival, Sayyid Mahmud Hayran of Akşehir, had ridden out against him on a lion, using a serpent for a whip. Hajji Bektash promptly proved his own superiority by sitting astride this rock and urging it into motion(32).

Dedebağı, a place with fruit and poplar trees, is another much-frequented site. It contains the tombs of revered figures, and a spring, and is a place where tiny stones resembling grains of wheat and lentils are to be found. These are highly prized as a cure for barrenness. Women swallow a 'wheat grain' for a son or a 'lentil' if they want a daughter. Tradition records that the grains were fossilised by Hajji Bektash.

Bigger stones are the central attraction at the site known as 'Beş Taş' (Five Stones). These are the five large rocks that are believed to have spoken to give evidence in favour of Hajji Bektash. Here the pilgrims may come in groups, sacrifice, cook meals in a cauldron, dance, pray and sing. Returning to the edge of the town the pilgrim may call at Kadıncık Evi, the house where Hajji Bektash is said to have lodged and which he later miraculously saved from collapse. The Alevi-Bektashis believe that Kadıncık became the wife of Hajji Bektash and bore him a son. The Yol Evladı vehemently reject this story but revere Kadıncık for offering hospitality and devoted service to Hajji Bektash.

Some kilometres away on the other side of the town stands a hill known as Mount Arafat, on and around which are some of the most important sacred sites. Near here is a cemetery now dominated by the mausoleum of the Çelebis who claim descent from Hajji Bektash. This was built in the mid-1970s. It is close to the waters of Zemzem, a fountain whose waters, 'colder than ice and sweeter than honey' are said to flow direct from Khurasan, whence Hajji Bektash originated. A few yards from here is a small, walled enclosure containing the grave of a devout Bektashi woman who died in 1968. She was known for achieving ecstatic states during tarikat ceremonies and it was her dearest wish to be buried at Hacıbektaş. Some visitors take soil from the top of this grave and swallow it when breaking their Muharram fast or to cure illness or barrenness(33).

Still around Mount Arafat the pilgrim may, as at Mecca, fling stones at 'demons' and follow a number of other traditions, the most important of which concerns the rock known as 'Çilehane'. This rock contains a small cave with an entrance big enough to admit a stooping man and with a hole a few feet from the ground through which a person of normal size may squeeze his way out headfirst. According to widespread Bektashi belief, this opening in the solid rock will close to prevent a sinful person - however slim - from passing through. Some say such a sinner would be crushed to death, others that a sacrifice made for him would secure his release. Conversely, the jaws of this rock will open wider to let a portly but worthy person pass through. The fame of this rock is known to Bektashis everywhere, and passing through the hole is taken very seriously by some of them; one of the first questions asked of any Bektashi returning from a visit to Hacibektas is, 'Did you get through the hole?' and an affirmative answer assures increased respect.

The attitude of prominent religious Bektashis to such practices is varied. Some observe them personally, others are not particularly interested in them but make no effort either to persuade or dissuade their followers and, with typical Bektashi tolerance, say it is entirely up to the individual whether he believes in such things or not. Within Bektashism tolerance, freedom of speech, love of mankind, wit, and generous hospitality remain highly cherished virtues. So, too, is education, though it must be admitted that only a few of the leaders now have sufficient learning to master the ancient teachings properly. (Hardly any can read the old script or understand Arabic, so the mystical significance of letters and numbers is but vaguely understood.) Nor are many of them well enough educated to put their views across convincingly to young people who have received a secular, scientific education.

Nevertheless, the thousands who flock to Hacibektas for the mid-August festival and the many who conscientiously visit the tekke and other sacred sites are proof that, despite the ban that has made the tarikat illegal since 1925, Bektashism is very far from dead. The military coup in 1980 halted political activity in Turkey and this has put a stop to open politicking at the Festival, which in 1981 was under the firm control of the kaymakam (district governor) and planned as a tourist attraction. But the activities of the religious Bektashis continued in private. They still dream that one day their Order will be permitted to operate openly and their dedebaba reinstated in the tekke then restored to its old function. That day, if it ever comes, is no doubt far away. In the meantime, Bektashism, capable of endless reinterpretations and shifts of emphasis, shows every intention of surviving, thereby adding to the variety of religious experience and continuing to be at the very centre of the lives of its devotees who find in it spiritual uplift and a refuge from the world that often treats them badly; within the Order they may find the fulfilment and even the advancement that elude them in the world outside, and their personalities may blossom and their self-respect be bolstered in an environment not governed by material considerations or dependent upon worldy success.

NOTES

1. In this article English spellings are used for Bektashi (modern Turkish Bektaşî) and the founding saint Hajji Bektash (Hacı Bektaş), but Turkish spelling is used for the place name Hacıbektaş and certain other words whose meaning is explained.
2. Tarikat is the modern Turkish form of the Arabic tariqa (a way, the term for a Sufi path; a mystical method or school of guidance for following the way).
3. F.W. Hasluck, Christianity and Islam Under the Sultans, 2 vols., (Oxford University Press, Oxford, 1929).
4. John Kingsley Birge, The Bektashi Order of Dervishes (London, 1937, reprinted 1965).
5. tekke, a Dervish lodge, main local meeting place of a Sufi order.
6. Birge, The Bektashi Order, p. 83.

7. Ali Sümer, Andoluda Türk Öncüsü Hacı Bektaş Velî (printed privately, Ankara, 1970) p. 83.
8. A. Celalettin Ulusoy, Hünkâr Hacı Bektaş Velî ve Alevî-Bektaşî Yolu (printed privately, Hacıbektaş, 1980) p. 261.
9. Ibid., p. 256.
10. The Alevis of Hamzababa, a mountain village near Turgutlu in S.W. Turkey, may be cited as a typical example of this. They enjoy close friendship with Bektashis, some of whom come to visit the tomb of Hamza Baba. A prominent Bektashi baba who died in 1981 was buried in Hamza Baba. But the inhabitants call themselves Alevis and do distinguish themselves from Bektashis.
11. Ulusoy, Hünkâr Hacı Bektaş, p. 187.
12. Birge, The Bektashi Order, pp. 132-4.
13. Ulusoy, Hünkâr Hacı Bektaş, p. 189.
14. Sümer, Anadoluda, p. 20.
15. (a) There is a small tekke in Tarsus that houses relics evacuated from Crete. These relics include a highly prized icon depicting ^cAli and Hajji Bektash. (b) An account appearing in Milliyet of 28th August 1979 refers to pictures hidden in Hajji Bektash's tomb in 1923.
16. An informant quoted in a Milliyet article of 28th August 1979 asserted that two pictures of Hajji Bektash, Balım Sultan, and Abdal Musa were said to be the Bektashi secret.
17. Ehl-i beyt - literally 'the family of the House of Muhammad', but interpreted by Bektashis to mean ^cAli and his children, as opposed to Ehl-i Sünni (Ar. ahl al-Sunna), the orthodox.
18. Hasluck, Christianity and Islam, pp. 165-6.
19. Gustav Thaiss, ' Religious Symbolism and Social Change', in Nikki R. Keddie (ed.), Scholars, Saints and Sufis, (University of California Press, California, 1972) p. 358.
20. Memet Faut, Pir Sultan Abdal (De Yayınevi, Istanbul, 1977) p. 7.
21. Birge, The Bektashi Order, p. 78.
22. Enver Behnan Şapolyo, Mezhepler ve Tarikatlar Tarihi (Türkiye Yayınevi, Istanbul, 1964) p. 440. (Unfortunately, this book, though interesting, contains contradictory information and is not a reliable guide).
23. Birge, The Bektashi Order, p. 81.
24. Ulusoy, Hünkâr Hacı Bektaş, pp. 99-104.
25. Law 677, 13th December, 1925, closed all Dervish lodges, prohibited the use of titles relating to positions in the tarikats, the wearing of tarikat costume, closed tombs sacred to the tarikats, and laid down penalties for contravention of these rules.
26. I have been fortunate enough to pay repeated visits to Hacıbektaş since 1969 and have attended most of the annual

Bektashis in Turkey

celebrations. I am pleased to acknowledge my gratitude to the
Centre for Middle Eastern and Islamic Studies, University of
Durham, for financial support that has enabled me to make
these visits, and to the people of Hacıbektas for their
exceptional hospitality, friendship and helpfulness.
   27. Hasluck, Christianity and Islam, p. 165.
   28. Sümer, Anadoluda, p. 27.
   29. This point has been stressed to me by several
people, including the late Cahit Öztelli, a distinguished
folklorist, with whom I attended the evening celebrations in
1977.
   30. This claim was made by the person many of the Yol
Evladi regard as their world leader. Asked for supporting
evidence, he replied 'They were honest, truthful and
courageous; these are the qualities of a Turk'.
   31. Hacıbektaş Turizm Derneği, Hacı Bektaş Veli
Bildiriler Denemeler Açıkoturum (Hacıbektas Turizm Derneği,
Ankara, 1977) p. 8.
   32. I am indebted to the Sufi scholar, Mr A.G.E. Blake,
for the information that this legend is almost identical to an
Indian tradition, relating to Janadeva (1275-1297), a
Naharashtran saint.
   33. Soil from around here, not necessarily from this
grave, is widely accepted as a substitute for soil from
Karbala used for the same purpose. See Bedri Noyan,
Hacıbektaş'ta Pîrevi ve Diğer Ziyaret Yerleri (printed
privately, Izmir, 1964) p. 68.

REFERENCES

Birge, J.K. (1937) The Bektashi Order of Dervishes, Luzac,
   London
Fuat, M. (1977) Pir Sultan Abdal, De Yayınevi, Istanbul
Hacıbektaş Turizm Derneği (1977) Hacı Bektaş Veli Bildiriler
   Denemeler Açıkoturum, Ankara
Hasluck, F.W. (1929) Christianity and Islam Under the
   Sultans, Oxford University Press, Oxford
Noyan, B. (1964) Hacıbektaş'ta Pîrevi ve Diğer Ziyaret
   Yerleri, Izmir
Sümer, A. (1970) Andoluda Türk Öncüsü Hacı Bektaş Veli,
   Ankara
Şapolyo, E.B. (1964) Mezhepler ve Tarikatlar Tarihi, Türkiye
   Yayınevi, Istanbul
Thaiss, G. (1972) 'Religious Symbolism and Social Change', in
   N.R. Keddie (ed.) Scholars, Saints and Sufis,
   University of California Press, California, pp. 349-366

THE SHI^CI ESTABLISHMENT IN MODERN IRAN

Denis MacEoin

Since 1978, the images of mullas, mujtahids and ayatollahs have flickered across our television screens and crammed the front pages of our newspapers. Shi^ci Islam, almost unknown before then to most people in the West, was suddenly thrust onto the centre stage of world events, where it has since played a leading role in the drama of international politics, economics and intrigue. The turbaned prelates of Tehran, once known in the Western world only to an esoteric cabal of academics, have become the stock-in-trade of political commentators, newscasters, cartoonists and even comedians, while terms such as 'ayatollah' have earned a permanent place in our dictionaries. A combination of genuinely thrilling incidents and unprecedented media coverage has made of the Islamic Revolution in Iran one of the most observed events in history. When, in April 1917, Lenin arrived at the Finland Station in Petrograd from exile in Switzerland, he was met by a large crowd, but there were no radio microphones or television cameras waiting to announce his coming to the world. In February 1979, from the moment Ayatollah Khumaini's jet left France to the moment it touched down at Mehrabad airport outside Tehran, the eyes of the world were on him. The eventual expulsion of most foreign journalists and the smothering of the Iranian press may have served to dull the world's vision, but its interest has slackened very little. The fall of the Shah, his later wanderings and death, the war with Iraq, the taking of the American hostages, the negotiations leading to their eventual release, the assassinations of leading politicians and clergymen, and the growth of internal dissension and repression, accompanied by mass executions, have all kept our attention focussed on Iran, and future developments are certain to claim it again.

To most people, however, the origins and motives of the Iranian revolution appear just as obscure now as they did in 1978. Events in Iran since then have been, at times, so alien and bizarre that they might as well have been taking place on another planet. The revolution took place in a context we can all readily understand: superpower rivalry, an oil-boosted economy, an excessive build-up of the armed forces and military hardware, internal political repression, rapid industrialization, the development of a centralized state structure with an unwieldy bureaucratic apparatus, the emergence of a diversified opposition, internal political repression, the creation of a single party system, and so on. But these factors, important as they may be, are all secondary in many respects to the central inspiration of the revolution: the growth of an articulate religious opposition.

In his book Iran: Dictatorship and Development(1), issued at the end of 1978 as the revolution was getting under way, the Marxist writer Fred Halliday showed penetrating insight into the economic, social and general political factors present in Iran on the eve of the revolution and dealt at length with various groups opposed to the Pahlavi regime, but scarcely mentioned the traditional religious opposition, the one force that, in the end, really mattered. This tendency to dismiss the forces of religious reaction was and still is a major factor distorting Western evaluations of the revolution and the spirit that animates it. But there is really very little excuse for such a head-in-the-sand attitude. Guenter Lewy(2) and others have demonstrated the very close links which have existed in the past and which exist today between religious ideologies and revolutionary movements. In the particular case of Iran, the problematic relationship of church and state has been closely examined by a number of scholars over the past twenty years. The nature of that relationship has been changed radically by the Islamic Revolution, but a survey of past developments is essential to an understanding of the present situation.

In order to arrive at such an understanding, it will be necessary to begin with a survey of some central features of Shi^ci Islam, and this will require us to go back, first of all, to the seventh century. This may seem a perverse and academic approach to a paper forming part of a collection on 'Aspects of Islam in the Modern World', but it is an essential beginning if we are to penetrate the thinking of Ayatollah Khumaini or comprehend the mentality of the clerical elite in control of modern Iran. For these are men whose religious and political ideas are moulded by events that took place as much as thirteen hundred years ago, for whom the seventh and eighth and ninth centuries are as close as yesterday. A survey of the main features of Shi^cism is also important in that many of our questions about the role of the clergy in the revolution may be answered by reference to the differences between Shi^cism and mainstream Islam.

There is, ideally, no distinction in Islam between church and state, religion and politics. The Prophet Muhammad is deemed to have brought from God not only a body of moral and ethical precepts as embodied in the Qur'an, but to have instituted a community of believers governed by him and subject in all affairs, both public and private, to the law of God derived from His Book and from the sayings and practice of His prophet. Islam is both religion and polity, ethic and action. Following the death of Muhammad in the year 632, a variety of theories were advanced as to who should lead the state or, in the process of time, the individual states of the Islamic world. The majority adopted a system of "elected" Caliphs, soon followed by hereditary dynasties of Caliphs and, before long, by semi-autonomous rulers subject to the Caliph in theory only. But a small party or shi^{c}a claimed that supreme authority should have passed directly to ^{c}Ali, a cousin and son-in-law of the Prophet, to descend in his line in perpetuity. Although ^{c}Ali did become Caliph in 656 and ruled until his assassination in 661, he was unable to establish hereditary rule in his line. The Muslim community was already seriously divided by then and, following the establishment of the Umayyad dynasty on ^{c}Ali's death, his eldest son Hasan was forced to abandon his claim to the Caliphate. Some years later, however, a younger son of ^{c}Ali, Husain, led a rebellion against the Caliph Yazid. Scarcely begun, the rebellion was crushed in 680, when Husain and a band of about seventy followers were surrounded at Karbala in modern Iraq and massacred almost to a man. It was here at Karbala that Shi^{c}ism had its true birth and it is in the passion of Husain that it continues to find the inner force that drives it. When, in the years leading up to the Revolution, Shi^{c}i preachers identified the Pahlavi dynasty with the Umayyads and Muhammad Reza Shah with the tyrant Yazid, they were not just playing with metaphors. They were drawing, as had their predecessors in earlier generations, on a deep-seated interpretation of the drama of history, in which changing events and persons play again and again the same basic roles, in which truth and justice are trampled underfoot by falsehood and tyranny, and in which the true ruler of mankind is denied his rights by a bloody usurper. Every year the drama of Husain is acted out in passion plays performed on the festival of his martyrdom, while lines of black-clothed men share in his sufferings as they whip themselves with chains and call on him for salvation. These images of passion and martyrdom recurred with fearful frequency during the winter of 1978-79.

In the early years of Islam, numerous claimants to the Caliphate appeared among the descendants of ^{c}Ali, some leading revolutionary movements and putting forward radical messianic claims. But through a son of Husain, surnamed Zain al-^{c}Abidin, who had survived the massacre of Karbala, a line of direct descendants, known to their followers as 'Imams', adopted a quietist position towards the state(3). To those who followed them they were still the true rulers, but this position was now expressed less in simple political terms or on the basis of physical descent and increasingly on the grounds of divine appointment or inspiration. Infallibly guided, they alone could guide the community in all affairs of state, law and religion. In later years, the doctrine of the Imamate was to be developed further still, to the point where the Imams came to be regarded as virtual manifestations of the divinity, as the causes of creation, informed of all things, alive from eternity, mediators between God and man. 'Whoso dies without knowing the Imam of his age', states one popular tradition, 'it is as if he had died before the coming of Islam'(4).

Out of the numerous Shi^{c}i sects of this early period, there developed a moderate, central position which forms the basis for the Shi^{c}ism of Iran today. In the year 872, the twelfth Imam, Muhammad al-Mahdi, the eleventh in direct descent from ^{c}Ali, disappeared in the city of Samarra at the age of five. His disappearance, which rapidly followed his father's death, remains unexplained, but his followers were quick to rationalize it by declaring that he had gone into 'occultation', a state in which he remained alive but invisible in this world. The charismatic leadership which he had provided was continued, however, in a semi-routinized form by a succession of four agents or 'gates', men who claimed to be channels of communication between the hidden Imam and his people. On the death of the last of these in 940, however, this system of representation abruptly ceased. The Imam, it is now said, had passed from a state of 'lesser occultation', in which he remained in communication with men through his gates, to a state of 'greater occultation', in which communication is extremely limited. He will return only at the end of the world, to bring peace and justice and establish a rule of righteousness on earth. Until then, however, he remains the true ruler of men, whose authority has been usurped by kings and princes and whose sovereignty is recognized by but a few.

Inspired by the twin themes of Husain's passion and the expectation of the parousia of the hidden Imam, Twelver Shi^{c}ism, as it came to be known (because of the number of its Imams), continued to exist as a quietist movement within the main body of Islam. Although other Shi^{c}i or quasi-Shi^{c}i groups - notably the Fatimids, Carmathians and Zaidis - obtained some measure of political power from about the 9th century, the Twelvers remained scattered and politically weak until the emergence of the Safavi dynasty in Iran at the beginning of the 16th century. Under the Safavis, Twelver Shi^{c}ism was made the state religion of the country. Widespread, largely forcible conversion took place (with the result that the Shi^{c}a today form well over 90 per cent of the Iranian population) and a centralized Shi^{c}i establishment was created under the patronage of the ruling house.

The Safavi state entered into rapid decline in the 17th

century, finally to collapse like a house of cards before an Afghan invasion in 1722. The territorial integrity of Iran remained in jeopardy during the anarchic sixty-year interregnum between then and the establishment of a new central state under the Qajar dynasty, destined to remain in power until 1925. The continuance of Shi^{c}ism as the established religion of the country was itself threatened during the unstable years of the 18th century, but a rapid reconsacration and reconsolidation followed the renaissance of national and religious life under the Qajars. The Safavi experience could not be repeated, however, as Iran, in common with most other Muslim countries, entered the sphere of European influence and came under powerful political, economic and cultural pressures. Like Muslims elsewhere, the Shi^{c}is of Iran were faced by new challenges to their moral, intellectual and spiritual traditions, but the distinctiveness of Shi^{c}ism coupled with the somewhat anomalous position of Iran vis-a-vis the Superpowers of the nineteenth century -- who bullied but never actually colonized it -- meant that their reactions to these challenges differed, sometimes radically, from those of their Sunni neighbours. The pressures of the late 19th century were much intensified during the rule of the Pahlavi dynasty, established by the former Reza Khan in 1925, and it is in the religious response to those pressures -- essentially those of Westernization, secularization, and rapid modernization on the one hand and the growth of internal political repression and control on the other -- that we must seek the origins of the events of recent years. The role of the religious institution in those events and its continuing role as the central power of the new Iranian state themselves owe much to the confluence of three important developments in Shi^{c}ism since the late Safavi period. These developements can best be examined under three headings: the growth of charismatically-based religious authority; the internal re-organization of the religious establishment; and the polarization of relations between the religious hierarchy and the state.

We have already observed that Shi^{c}ism came into being as a movement centred around the question of authority over the community of believers, and in the absence of the Imam it became the central concern of that community to identify and legitimize authority in a situation where charisma could no longer be 'transmitted' to (or 'focussed' on) a single individual. The legitimation took several forms, one of the most important of which was that the role and status of the Shi^{c}i clergy, the ^{c}ulama, were defined and accorded increasing importance. During the lifetimes of the Imams, the influence of the Shi^{c}i clergy had been considerably restricted by the presence on earth of a supreme centre of authority, but the vacuum created by the Imam's absence gave them scope to develop in both theory and practice the basis for their own authority over the faithful. This authority was much enhanced following the establishment of Twelver Shi^cism under the Safavis, whose royal patronage raised the power, prestige and influence of the Shi^ci clergy to heights beyond the reach of their Sunni counterparts and comparable only to the authority enjoyed by the heads of the major Sufi brotherhoods in the Ottoman Empire and North Africa. This access of power led, as we shall see, to serious tensions between the clergy and the later Safavi state, but, for the present, it will be useful to concentrate on the implications of this development within the religious hierarchy itself. By the end of the Safavi period, one group in particular among the clergy had risen to eminence. Known as mujtahids, these were individuals famed for their piety and learning and deemed capable of exercising independent judgment in matters of religious law. Whereas in Sunni Islam authority to act thus is generally considered to have ceased in the third Islamic century, and all believers are required to obey the opinions laid down by then, according to Twelver Shi^ci theory such judgment may still be exercised by a small number of outstanding clergy in every generation. In practice, the authority of the Qur'an and religious tradition is such that considerable restrictions are placed on their freedom to deviate from established practices in any but minor points. The principle itself, however, is sufficient to ensure the authority of the mujtahids in the community.

A further impetus to the development of this spiritual authority came during the late eighteenth century, in the years leading up to the Qajar restoration. Large numbers of clergy had taken refuge from the convulsions of Iran in the Shi^ci shrine centres of Najaf, Karbala and Samarra in Ottoman-controlled Iraq. This concentration of clergy in one area led to an important theological debate, one of whose major consequences was the definite establishment of the mujtahids as supreme authorities in Shi^cism. The subsequent creation of a new Shi^ci state in Iran under the Qajars provided an opportunity for them to exercise their power and saw the institutionalization of their positions in the concept of the marja^c al-taqlid ('source of imitation'), a term used to describe a mujtahid deemed to be endowed with overriding authority in religious matters, by virtue of his learing, his piety and, above all else, his popularity as expressed in the size of his following. The faithful in general and, indeed, other scholars, are obliged to follow the legal rulings of one among the several men who rise to this rank, hence the title 'source of imitation'. Only a few of these 'sources of imitation' emerge in any generation, some half dozen only being recognized as such at present.

Although charismatic authority such as that exercised by the 'source of imitation' may be spread over a body of individuals, there seems to be a tendency towards the emergence of a single <u>marja^c</u> as supreme bearer of that authority. Shi^{c}ism was, as we have seen, built around the unchallengeable charismatic authority of the Imam. As the nineteenth century progressed, we can observe a growing tendency to echo this by singling out exceptional individuals as 'sources of imitation' over very wide areas, leading to the recognition of Shaikh Muhammad Hasan al-Najafi (d.1850) as the sole authority of his day. Al-Najafi's pupil, Shaikh Murtada Ansari (d.1864-65) succeeded to this supreme position, being acknowledged as an authority not only in Iran and Iraq, but in Turkey, Arabia and India. More significantly, there are indications that he was recognized as 'the first general vicegerent' of the Imam. This term has since been applied to a number of leading <u>maraji^c</u> and has acquired quasi-messianic connotations in respect to Ayatollah Khumaini. The political implications of this concept should be clear in the light of what we have said earlier concerning the authority of the Imam as the sole legitimate ruler of the community. As his representative, the supreme religious leader must, in his turn, be in a position to claim a similar authority -- a condition which, as we shall see, contributed greatly to tension between the state and claimants to spiritual power.

The stage seemed to be set in the late nineteenth century for the routinization of the charisma of the single <u>marja^c</u> in a permanent office with a formalized principle of succession but, although attempts along these lines were made, nothing substantial was achieved. Following the death in 1895 of Mirza Hasan Shirazi, who had been sole 'source of imitation' since about 1865, there was no agreement as to the most worthy successor and, since then, there has been only sporadic re-emergence of the concept, most notably in the person of Hajj Aqa Husain Burujirdi, who died in 1961. An apparent attempt to institutionalize the role of the <u>marja^c</u> may be seen, however, in the adoption of the title 'ayatollah' (<u>ayat Allah</u>: the sign of God), which has been applied to the leading <u>maraji^c</u> since the early years of this century. This term seems to have acquired a particular application to high ranking clerics adopting an oppositional role towards the government, a usage which clearly derives from the political implications of the role of the <u>marja^c</u>, to which we have referred above. From the time of Ayatollah Burujirdi, the term '<u>ayat Allah al-^{c}uzma</u>' (the greatest sign of God) has been used of the supreme 'source of imitation' and is currently applied to Ayatollah Khumaini in that capacity. In general, however, lack of a clearly regulated hierarchical system is, as we shall see, a persistent feature of Shi^{c}ism, and this tendency towards informal, charismatic modes of leadership has, so far, proved a sufficient counterbalance to the common tendencies of routinization and legalization. The question has become critical again, however, since the appearance of Ayatollah Khumaini, and we shall look at this matter once more when we come to examine more recent developments. An interesting and dramatic sidelight is cast on this tendency towards supreme charismatic leadership by two closely-linked heterodox movements which appeared in Shi^{c}ism in the middle of the nineteenth century -- Babism and Baha'ism. There is no space here to make more than a passing reference to the topic, but I believe that further research into the origins of these two sects may uncover much that is suggestive about the direction of charismatic authority in Iran as it stood on the verge of the modern period.

Beginning in 1844 as a reactionary messianic movement within Shi^{c}ism, Babism had, by 1848, attempted the abrogation of the Islamic legal system and, within another year, proclaimed the replacement of Islam by a new divine revelation. This extraordinary development, which was cut short by the physical repression of the Babis by 1852, was based on a series of claims to original charismatic authority by the founder of the movement, Sayyid ^{c}Ali Muhammad Shirazi, the Bab. Although he finally claimed to be a divine 'manifestation' sent by God with a new book and law, Shirazi had commenced his mission by urging no greater claim than that of representative or 'gate' (bab) of the Imam -- something not very far removed from what was later asserted of the supreme marja^c or what is today claimed for Khumaini by many of his followers. Baha'ism, which emerged out of Babism in the 1860's, was based on a similar claim to divine authority superseding that of the past, and achieved an even further-reaching charismatic breakthrough. In the end, the Baha'is claimed for their movement the status of a new religion, independent of Islam, a claim which has been furthered to some extent by the relative success of their missionary enterprises outside Iran throughout this century.

Apart from their undoubted intrinsic interest, Babism and Baha'ism seem to me to be significant in the present context for a number of reasons. It is, first of all, worth noting that, although nineteenth-century Islam witnessed the emergence of several messianic movements, such as the Mahdiyya of the Sudan or the Ahmadiyya in India, all of these remained within the bounds of Islam, from their own point of view, at least. It was only in Shi^{c}i Iran that a movement appeared which broke entirely from Islam and, in the end, successfully established itself as a new and, in some areas, even a rival religion. Although this phenomenon owes much to features typical of Shi^{c}ism throughout its history, there can be no question that it emerged out of tensions which also contributed towards modern developments within the orthodox clerical establishment, notably in the area of charismatic authority. Carried to an extreme degree, such authority threatened the entire edifice of Shi^{c}i orthodoxy. Baha'ism presented a particular challenge because it made explicit a problem which many Muslim scholars have confronted but seldom articulated during the last century and more since the pressures of modernization have called for some kind of reform within Islam. To justify certain reforms can be extremely difficult in an Islamic context, particularly where they seem to contradict the explicit text of the Qur'an or established tradition. The problem, quite simply, was to determine who could claim authority to make wholesale changes in the divine law or, indeed, whether such changes were permissible at all. The Baha'i solution was, of course, both the simplest and the least acceptable -- the advent of a new prophet, book, and laws. The general tendency of the Shi^{c}i clergy during this century to resist reform has almost certainly much to do with their perception of the dangers inherent in any attempt to abrogate the existing Islamic legal code.

It is, moreover, important to realize that it was Babism, not the recent revolution, which broke with the centuries-old Twelver commitment to political quietism by resorting to militant action in support of its claims. The quietism of the Imams after Husain had for its corollary the intense hope that a Mahdi or Qa'im would arise before long to avenge their wrongs, topple the government of the wicked, and establish the rule of justice on earth. In time, this Qa'im was identified with the twelfth Imam, who would arise in arms on his reappearance after occultation. The Babis expected this event to take place in 1845 and, although their hopes were disappointed in that year, the Bab's announcement that he was the Qa'im in person led to a series of bloody clashes between his followers and government forces in several parts of Iran. The Babi attempt to establish a theocratic government is a paradigm for the events of 1979 to 1980, in which a less explicit millenarianism played an important part. Strictly speaking, armed rebellion can only be justified in Shi^{c}ism by the appearance or near appearance of the Qa'im -- a point which, as the Babi experience shows, poses serious problems for the ^{c}ulama today. The fierce persecution of Baha'is which has occurred under the present regime has numerous motives, among which is, I think, a recognition on the part of the religious leadership that, although the sect has categorically repudiated militant action in favour of a return to the original Shi^{c}i policy of quietism and cooperation with the state, it retains the long-term aim of establishing theocratic rule in Iran and throughout the world. In this respect, it must inevitably be regarded as a group whose aims are ultimately incompatible with those of the revolution, because they are, in many ways, extremely close to them. This in itself serves to make clearer some of the tensions that have contributed to and continue to exist in the present Islamic state. In order to understand more clearly the context in which developments such as the move towards the emergence of a supreme marja^c took place, it will be necessary to look briefly at the organizational basis of the Shi^{c}i establishment. I have already mentioned that the most distinctive feature of the religious institution in Iran is its lack of highly routinized modes of leadership. There is a hierarchy, but there are few well-defined boundaries of function and authority, no universally-recognized system of grading, and no regularly-controlled method for advancement or succession. The process whereby a scholar rises to a position of eminence, acquiring a reputation as an ^{c}alim, than a mujtahid, and then, perhaps, as a marja^c al-taqlid follows no pre-determined system. The factors that count are the individual's learning and piety, the reputation of his teachers, the popularity of his books, the numbers of students attending his classes, the numbers of the faithful having recourse to his judgments, and so on. This lack of a wholly rationalized eccleasiastical organization has proved a crucial factor in allowing the Shi^{c}i clergy to preserve their independence even within the context of a Shi^{c}i state and is a matter of singular importance for the understanding of recent events.

In this connection, it is crucial to note the existence of a state of tension between those forces working to preserve this traditional lack of organization and developments tending towards a measure of rationalization. Thus, for example, entry to the ranks of the ^{c}ulama has traditionally been open to any capable individual, regardless of background, and many young men from poor families, particularly in rural areas, have sought this path as a means to social advancement, a few rising to become mujtahids. From the late Safavi period on, however, we can observe a process whereby religious authority passed not only from teacher to pupil but from father to son as well; descendants of leading scholars came to occupy positions of importance in the religious hierarchy with increasing frequency. Not only was the power of the individual scholar increasing, but the influence of certain clerical families was growing. Intermarriage between the members of these families strengthened this power to a degree that made entry into the higher echelons of the ^{c}ulama class increasingly difficult for those outside this power structure, though, as we have noted, far from impossible. This phenomenon of intermarriage among clerical families is still a major feature of the institution. Michael Fischer has indicated that all seven first-rank 'sources of imitation' of 1975 could be placed together in a single genealogical table which also included over two generations five other first-rank 'sources', four 'sources' of second rank, six other leading scholars, and extended connections to numerous other 'sources' and scholars(5).

I have previously noted that, following the collapse of the Safavi state in 1722, the Shi^{c}i religious institution established its spiritual and organizational centre at the shrine towns of Iraq. It was not until the twentieth century that any attempt was made to re-establish a viable spiritual capital for Shi^{c}ism within Iran itself. This was achieved by the re-creation of a hawza-yi ^{c}ilmi or collection of religious colleges at Qom. This city, the site of a major Shi^{c}i shrine, had been of some importance under the Safavis but, following their disappearance, it had declined greatly and had not recovered its prestige under the Qajars. Religious scholarship at the more advanced levels was carried on almost exclusively at the shrine centres of Najaf and Karbala. In 1916, however, Ayatollah Faid Qummi, followed by other scholars, returned to Qom to reclaim the old seminary buildings for renewed use as theological schools. In 1920, Shaikh ^{c}Abd al-Karim Ha'iri Yazdi arrived in Qom, leading an exodus back to Iran of Shi^{c}i clergy concerned about their position under the British mandate in Iraq. In subsequent years, other leading scholars also arrived in Qom to contribute towards its re-emergence as a centre of Shi^{c}i studies, a process which received tremendous impetus with the arrival there in 1945 of Ayatollah Hajj Sayyid Aqa Husain Burujiridi, one of the leading figures of modern Shi^{c}ism. Shortly after his arrival there, the chief Shi^{c}i mujtahid, Sayyid Abu'l-Hasan Isfahani died and, within two years, Burujirdi had succeeded to the position of sole 'source of imitation', a rank he was to hold until his own death in 1961. Apart from his achievements as a scholar, Burujirdi was responsible for a major re-organization of affairs in Qom, particularly in the theological schools, where he introduced formal courses, set books and even annual examinations in an attempt to regularize the system and raise the prestige of the theological colleges. His own role as chief cleric was much enhanced by the introduction of regular administrative practices, leading to a sense of increased co-ordination and effectiveness within the structure of the religious hierarchy. This is particularly reflected by the existence in Qom of an informal body of some thirty to forty mujtahids whose judgment is widely regarded as decisive in the matter of selecting a supreme 'source of imitation'.

Alongside this restructuring of the religious institution, we may observe the development of organizations for the propagation of Shi^{c}ism both inside and outside Iran. In 1943, ^{c}Ata Allah Shihabpur founded the Anjuman-i Tablighat-i Islami (Association for Islamic Propaganda) with branches throughout Iran, for the purpose of undertaking a wide-ranging publishing and preaching programme. Of greater significance was the establishment in Qom in 1965 of the Dar al-Tabligh al-Islami (Institute for the Propagation of Islam) under the direction of Ayatollah Muhammad Kazim Shari^catmadari, following the wishes of Ayatollah Burujirdi that such a centre be set up. Related to this activity, which sought to train young men in the faith who would then spread active commitment to Islam among the masses and even undertake missionary work abroad, was the emergence in the 1960's of what has been described as a 'religious counter-culture' exemplified in the writings of university-educated laymen and a number of clerics devoted to the exposition of Islam in terms of modern thought. Notable among these were ^cAli Shari^cati, Sayyid Mahmud Taliqani, and Mahdi Bazargan. Betwwen 1959 and 1962, a group of ^culama began to publish lectures in a monthly journal called Guftar-i Mah and established in Tehran a mosque and Islamic teaching centre known as the Husainiyya Irshad. Other journals and propaganda institutes followed, providing a ready platform for the ideas of prominent lay preachers, including some of those mentioned above. The influence of these writers and lecturers on the younger generation proved considerable and was a major factor in creating an ideological base for the revolutionary movement that overthrew the Pahlavis.

That revolutionary movement was not, however, a creation of the 1970's but rather the culmination of an ideological development that began in the earliest period of Shi^cism. We have already noted that there is no real distinction between religion and politics in Islam and that Shi^cism itself began as a politico-religious movement centred on the question of true authority within the community. We have seen how, in the period following the occultation of the Imam, the Shi^ci clergy developed the theory of their own authority over the faithful, based largely on their claim to be the general representatives of the will of the Imam. It is of particular significance for later trends that this development took place during a period when there was no fully-fledged, centralized and stable state in which Twelver Shi^cism was the established religion. This and the fact that Shi^ci scholars remained scattered in several countries throughout the Middle East meant that they preserved a large measure of independence from the demands which would have been imposed upon them had they been expected to function within a wholly Shi^ci context in a single state system and that they were free of the hierarchical needs of a church-like structure that would be imposed by a centralized clerical institution. This situation was radically altered by the establishment of Shi^cism under the Safavis. As we have seen, under the patronage of this dynasty the power and influence of the clergy were considerably enhanced. It was inevitable, however, that establishment would generate new tensions for them, tensions that nothing in their historical experience had taught them to resolve. In the absence of a Shi^ci state, it had been easy to formulate a theory of the illegitimacy of all government save that of the divinely-appointed and divinely-guided Imam or his representative. The direct government of the Imam might rest in abeyance, but the hope of his return and the establishment of divine justice under his rule could sustain and hearten the faithful living in countries governed by Sunnis or Shi^ci heretics. Now, here was a powerful Shi^ci state ruled by a dynasty of kings claiming descent from the seventh Imam and asserting their divine right to govern. In such circumstances, what was to be the attitude of the clergy, the Imam's true representatives, and how, indeed, were they to instruct their flocks?

In the end, the clergy divided into two main parties on this issue. There was, on the one hand, a body of clerics directly or indirectly appointed by the Shah, under the supreme religious authority of the state, the Sadr al-^cUlama. In contrast to this group of what were, in effect, state officials, stood the mujtahids, the charismatic basis for whose power we have already described. It was among this second group that the theory of the illegitimacy of the secular state -- of any secular state, Sunni or Shi^ci -- was raised almost to the status of a fundamental doctrine of the faith. During the early Safavi period, the balance of power between these two groups remained approximately equal, but in the later period, as the power of the state itself grew weaker, the mujtahids increased greatly in influence, with the authority of certain outstanding individuals almost counterbalancing that of the monarch. We have already seen that, during the late eighteenth century, their theoretical power was greatly increased and that the Qajar period saw it focussed in the persons of the 'sources of imitation'.

In the Sunni world during the nineteenth century, notably in the Ottoman Empire and Egypt, the development of highly centralized states had led to a marked lowering of the influence of the ^culama and other religious institutions such as the Sufi orders. In Iran, however, where a combination of social and geographical factors worked against the extension of central government control, the clergy not only retained but even strengthened their power(6). Traditionally, individual scholars, particularly in the provinces, had acted as representatives of the masses in oppostion to local or national government policies, but their regrouping through the Qajar period gave them greater collective strength. The power qf the clergy as a largely independent focus of authority within the Qajar state was dramatically revealed towards the end of the reign of Nasir al-Din Shah (assassinated 1896). Nasir al-Din had attempted to integrate the religious establishment within the state structure by appointing certain individuals to clerical positions subsidized by government patronage, but he was unable to bring the leading religious authorities into this system.

In 1890, he granted an English company a wide-ranging concession which gave them a monopoly of the curing and sale of tobacco in Iran. Indignation was widespread at what was seen as a further move on the part of the government to solicit the interference of an imperial power at the expense of national independence, and in 1891 agitation for the repeal of the concession surfaced throughout the country. A coalition of merchants and clergy in all the leading towns voiced their opposition to the measure, but their protests had little impact at first. In December 1891, however, a religious ruling was issued in the name of Mirza Hasan Shirazi, then sole marja^c al-taqlid, resident at Samarra in Iraq. In this ruling, the use of tobacco in any form was denounced as forbidden under religious law and all Shi^cis were summoned to abandon it. The effect was immediate and striking. Throughout Iran, no-one bought, sold or smoked tobacco and, within a month, the government was brought to its knees and forced to repeal the concession(7).

The power of the clergy as a centre of opposition to the state and its policies was further demonstrated in the course of the agitation which led to the granting of a constitution by Muzaffar al-Din Shah in 1906. Seeing a constitution as a means of restricting the previously unlimited power of the monarch, the majority of Shi^ci clerics joined with the merchant class and with a motley collection of reformers and liberals who sought to establish democratic government in Iran. It was through clerical influence that the 1906 Constitution contained the following statement in its second Article:

> At no time must any legal enactment of the Sacred National Consultative Assembly, established by the favour and assistance of His Holiness the Imam of the Age...; the favour of His Majesty the Shahinshah of Islam...; the care of the Proofs of Islam (the ^culama)... and the whole people of the Persian nation, be at variance with the sacred principles of Islam or the laws established by His Holiness the Best of Mankind.... It is hereby declared that it is for the learned doctors of theology... to determine whether such laws as may be proposed are or are not conformable to the principles of Islam....

It was enacted that a permanent committee of five mujtahids or other clergy be appointed from a list of twenty and empowered to reject any proposed piece of legislation considered at variance with Islamic law. The decisions of this committee were to remain binding until the return of the hidden Imam(8).

In theory, at least, the clergy were now set to play an even greater role in the government of Iran, their de facto power of veto being now enshrined in the Constitution establishing a national parliament. In practice, however, the troubles that were endemic during the last years of the Qajars prevented parliament from functioning properly, while the establishment of the Pahlavi dynasty by Reza Shah in 1925 transferred real power back into the hands of the monarch. Under the rule of Reza Shah, the clergy were to see their newly-gained power and prestige crumble inexorably under the onslaught of a determined programme of modernization and centralization. In imitation of Attaturk, Reza Shah embarked on a policy designed to drag Iran into the twentieth century and, like Attaturk, he perceived the clergy to be the major repository of traditionalism, obscurantism and reaction. He instituted a series of direct attacks on clerical power, including the abolition in 1928 of Islamic dress for all but a limited number of registered ^{c}ulama, the prohibition in 1929 of religious processions in the month of Muharram, and the compulsory unveiling of women in 1935. More far-reaching, however, were the consequences of the new Shah's introduction in 1928 of a Civil Code limiting severely the role of the religious law and the function of the clergy as its administrators together with the spread of secular education in place of the old clerical school system and the stress placed on nationalism instead of religion as a focus for the loyalty of the masses. Clerical opposition to these measures was muted and ineffective, particularly after the exile to Khurasan in 1929 of Reza Shah's leading parliamentary critic, Sayyid Hasan Mudarris, a leading cleric from Isfahan.

Following Reza Shah's abdication on the insistence of the Allies in 1941, the situation changed once more in favour of the clergy. The new Shah, Muhammad Reza, was as yet weak and needed to court the favour of the clergy in view of their continuing popularity with the people. The veil, albeit in a modified form, made its reappearance on the streets, Muharram processions were resumed, and, after the war, religious exiles, including Ayatollah Sayyid Abu'l-Qasim Kashani, re-entered the country. Clerical involvement in the events of 1951-53 was a significant factor both in Musaddiq's rise to power and in his eventual downfall. Ayatollah Kashani (d.1962) was a demagogue with a strong power base in the bazaar sector who had remained politically inactive during the reign of Reza Shah but now emerged as a leading figure in nationalist politics. He controlled a delegation of ^{c}ulama in the Majlis which acted as the parliamentary representatives of a wider organization, the Mujahidin-i Islam, under the nominal leadership of Shams Qanatabadi, while his popularity as a preacher enabled him to rally mass support to the nationalist cause of Musaddiq. In 1953, however, Kashani broke with the latter and, joining forces with Sayyid Muhammad Bihbahani, gave support to the CIA-sponsored coup which brought

Muhammad Reza Shah back to power. It is worth mentioning that, during this same period, a new dimension was added to the conflict between religion and state with the emergence of the Fida'iyan-i Islam, a reactionary terrorist group founded in 1943 by Sayyid Mujtaba Mirlawhi. Although crushed in 1955 by the arrest of numerous members and the execution of the Fida'iyan leadership, this group stands as a forerunner of later religiously-motivated terrorist movements, some of which played a major role in the events of 1978-79.

The crisis of the Musaddiq period had revealed to Muhammad Reza Shah the continuing power of the clergy to influence events, and for some time he adopted a policy of conciliation towards them. In 1955-56, the government allowed some of the clergy, led by Mulla Muhammad Taqi Falsafi, to conduct a pogrom against the Baha'i religious minority. Government officials such as Taymur Bakhtiyar, the military governor of Tehran, and Prime Minister Asad Allah ^{c}Alam cooperated in the attack, which involved the partial destruction of the Baha'i national headquarters in the capital, while Ayatollah Burujirdi expressed approval of the measures taken. In the end, international pressure forced the government to withdraw its support for overt persecution, although less open forms of discrimination were allowed to continue throughout the rest of the Pahlavi period, paving the way for a more devastating pogrom since the Islamic revolution. On a more positive level, the Shah took pains to cultivate a small group of clerics willing to cooperate with the government, led by Ayatollah Muhammad Bihbahani and Sayyid Hasan Imami, the Imam-Jum^{c}a (leading state-appointed cleric) of Tehran, together with some thirty-five provincial Imam-Jum^{c}a's and the co-operation of leading mujtahids such as Ayatollah Shahab al-Din Mar^{c}ashi and Ayatollah Sayyid Muhammad Kazim Shari^{c}atmadari.

As the power of the regime was gradually reasserted, however, opposition again began to mount and, in 1963, Ayatollah Ruhollah Khumaini began to preach against the government in the Faidiyya theological school at Qom. Khumaini has generally been represented as attacking at this point land reform and female enfranchisement, but Hamid Algar suggests that the real targets of his criticism were:

> autocratic rule and violation of the constitution; the proposal to grant capitulatory rights to American advisors and military personnel in Iran and their dependants; the contracting of a $200 million loan from the United States for the purchase of military equipment; and the maintenance of diplomatic, commercial, and other relations with Israel, a state hostile to the Muslims and Islam.(9)

Later developments confirm that the political interests of the

clergy were now widening and that purely reactionary motives
were playing a less significant role in their opposition to
government policies. Official attempts to suppress Khumaini's
protests led in June 1963 to serious disturbances in Mashhad,
Qom, Tehran, Shiraz, and elsewhere, in which demonstrations
were organized by local clergy. In the end, the government
succeeded in quelling the disturbances with the loss of
possibly thousands of lives. Khumaini himself was arrested
and exiled, first to Turkey, then, in 1965, to Najaf in Iraq,
where he became a centre for opposition to the Pahlavi
regime.

In the meantime, internal developments within the
religious establishment were becoming entangled with the
political situation in Iran. Following the death in 1961 of
Ayatollah Burujirdi, the Shah had given clear indications that
he would favour the appointment as supreme marja^c and
Ayatollah al-^{c}Uzma of Ayatollah Shaikh Muhsin Hakim, a
politically quietist cleric living at Najaf. Although Ayatollah
al-Hakim was well regarded, the Shah's intervention was itself
a factor militating against his general recognition and instead
three mujtahids emerged as more or less equal heirs to
Burujirdi: Ayatollah Muhammad Hadi Milani in Mashhad,
Ayatollah Sayyid Muhammad Kazim Shari^{c}atmadari in Qom, and
Ayatollah Sayyid Ruhollah Khumaini in Najaf. On the death of
Shaikh Muhsin al-Hakim in 1970, the Shah made the mistake of
seeking to use it as a second opportunity to encourage the
recognition of an offically approved supreme 'source of
imitation'. The Shah's ploy backfired more seriously this time
when forty-eight clerics in Qom sent a telegram to Ayatollah
Khumaini offering condolences on the death of Shaikh Muhsin
and presenting their allegiance to him. Although this was by
no means tantamount to general recognition of Khumaini as
Ayatollah al-^{c}Uzma -- Shari^{c}atmadari, for example, was
regarded as unquestionably more learned -- the trend of later
events served to increase his authority, and his role during
and after the revolution has secured him absolute power
throughout the Shi^{c}i world.

That Khumaini should now be regarded as Ayatollah
al-^{c}Uzma and as the representative of the Imam, and that he
should be the first mujtahid to head a state, is not merely
due to his political role, however. As a political reality, it
cannot be divorced from the ideological theories developed by
him in his writings, notably in his collection of lectures
entitled Wilayat-i faqih(10). It would be outside the scope of
the present paper to attempt even a brief survey of
Khumaini's thought, but a few points of particular relevance
deserve to be brought out. It is fundamental to his political
outlook that the religious leaders, in their capacity as experts
in the sacred law (fuqaha, sing. faqih) and as mujtahids
empowered to exercise independent reasoning, are the sole
legitimate sources of ruling authority in a Shi^{c}i state,

inasmuch as they and they alone are the true successors of the Prophet and the Imams(11). As such, they possess the same authority to rule as the latter:

> This notion that the governing powers of the Prophet were greater than those of the Amir (^{c}Ali) or that the governing powers of the Amir were greater than those of the faqih is false and mistaken. Undoubtedly, the endowments of the Prophet are greater than those of all the world and, after him, those of the Amir are greater than all; but abundance of spiritual endowments does not increase powers of government. God has granted the same powers and guardianship (wilayat) which were possessed by the Prophet and the Imams... to the present government (i.e. that of the clergy), except that no one individual is specified; there is simply the term: 'a just scholar'(12). In other words: 'the true rulers are the fuqaha' '.(13)

Although Khumaini is somewhat ambivalent about whether wilayat is to be exercised by one faqih or several, his own charismatic authority as standard-bearer of the revolution and Ayatollah al-^{c}Uzma coupled with the existing theory of supreme marja^c has meant that, in practice, he has become the Wali-yi Faqih (Guardian and Jurisprudent) at the head of the state. This principle of a single faqih was, in fact, enshrined in the new Iranian Constitution by an amendment issued in November 1979 by the Council of Experts (Majlis-i Khibrigan) set up to finalize the draft constitution of June. According to this amendment, the highest authority in the country was to be the Wali-yi Faqih, who would be supreme commander of the armed forces, with powers to appoint or dismiss all high-ranking officers; he would also have powers to appoint or dismiss members of the higher judiciary; to declare war and conclude peace; to give prior approval to candidates for the presidency; to dismiss the President if so reommended by the Supreme Court or National Assembly; to reduce or annul prison sentences; and to appoint six clerical members to an 11-member Council of Guardians. He would represent the legitimacy of the regime and be able to intervene directly or through the Council of Guardians in all affairs of state. Should there be no generally acknowledged spiritual authority -- a recognition of the present realities of the method of selecting a supreme marja^c -- wilayat would be exercised by a college of ^{c}ulama. This amendment was approved by a referendum held on 2-3 December 1979, and in 1982 it was formally established that the college of ^{c}ulama would take charge following the death of Khumaini.

It would be a rash observer indeed who would venture to plot the course of events in the ever-changing tangle of incidents and personalities of modern Iran. Unquestionably, the clergy have risked everything on the revolution. Should their excesses cause it to fall, they will fall with it, perhaps never to rise again. If, however, it should endure in some form and their power within the state remain supreme, it is inevitable that the character of their organization and authority will be radically changed, as is already implicit in the doctrine of wilayat-i faqih. They will become a ruling class with a routinized structure. It is almost certain that the internal organization of the clerical establishment, begun by Burujirdi and others in Qom, will be speeded up and the hierarchical system rationalized. This process is likely to begin at the top once Khumaini dies. At present, the weakest point in the regime's power structure is excessive reliance on the charismatic authority of Khumaini, which has a strongly original quality. When he dies, he will leave a void which will not easily be filled. Ayatollah Mahmud Taliqani was originally Khumaini's most likely successor, but his death some months after the revolution left an important gap. Some see Ayatollah Husain Muntazari as the most probable candidate, but it is certain that his succession would be bitterly disputed. Shari^{c}atmadari was officially declared bereft of his title of Ayatollah following his implication in the Qutbzada plot of early 1982, and is now too old and politically weak to offer a serious challenge to the more extreme section of the clergy. Reliance on ad hoc methods from the past would be bound to lead Iran even further into a state of anarchy, but undue routinization would allow the introduction of more mundane factors into the equation, and it is conceivable that this would lead to a second phase of religious opposition.

The Shi^{c}i clergy have been presented with a challenge unique in their history and unusual enough, indeed, in the history of any people. Their response to that challenge so far has not been encouraging. The totalitarianism inherent in any system seeking a wholesale reconstruction of society along predetermined ideological lines has issued, inevitably, in a wave of repression and bloodshed. The form taken by the revolution has not been accidental. I trust that I have shown that it has its roots in the very depths of Shi^{c}i history and thought. In the end, the values of the Iranian revolution are not, for the most part, values that the majority of us can share. But much will have been achieved if we are, at least, able to understand them.

NOTES

1. Harmondsworth, 1979. The book actually appeared in late 1978.
2. See Religion and Revolution, (New York, 1974).
3. On the development of this quietist or 'legitimist' line, see S.H.M. Jafri, The Origins and Early Development of Shi^{c}a Islam (London and New York, 1979), chapters 8, 9,

10,11.
4. Abu Ja^{c}far Muhammad al-Kulaini, Rawdat al-Kafi (Najaf, 1385/1965-66), p.129.
5. Iran pp.91-92.
6. Cf. N.R. Keddie, 'The Roots of the Ulama's Power in Modern Iran' in idem., (ed.), Scholars, Saints, and Sufis (Berkeley, Los Angeles, London, 1972) pp.212-13.
7. On the 'tobacco rebellion' see idem., Religion and Rebellion in Iran, the tobacco protest of 1891-1892 (London, 1966).
8. Text quoted in E.G. Browne, The Persian Revolution 1905-1909 (Cambridge, 1910), pp.372-73.
9. 'The Oppositional Role of the Ulama in Twentieth-Century Iran' in Keddie Scholars, p.246.
10. First published Najaf, 1971.
11. Wilayat-i faqih, Persian trans. (Tehran, 1978), pp.74-89.
12. Ibid., p.84.
13. Ibid., p.60.

REFERENCES

Algar, H. (1969) Religion and State in Iran 1785-1906, Berkeley and Los Angeles
Idem., (1972) 'The Oppositional Role of the Ulama in Twentieth-Century Iran' in N.R. Keddie (ed.) Scholars, Saints, and Sufis, Berkeley, Los Angles, London
Idem., 'Iran' under 'Islah' Encyclopaedia of Islam (2nd ed.)
Amanat, A. (1981) 'The Early Years of the Babi Movement', unpublished Ph.D. dissertation, Oxford
Avery, P. (1965) Modern Iran, London
Bagley, F.R.C. (1970, 1972) 'Religion and state in modern Iran', Part 1, Actes du Ve Congres international d'arabisants et islamisants, Brussels, pp.75-88; Part 2, Proceedings of the VIth Congress of Arabic and Islamic Studies, Stockholm, pp.31-44
Idem., (1974) 'Some suggestions for future research on modern Shi^{c}ism', Akten des VII Kongresses fur Arabistik und Islamwissenschaft, Gottingen, pp.59-65
Bill, J.A. (1972) The Politics of Iran: Groups, Classes and Modernization, Columbus, Ohio
Binder, L. (1965) 'The Proofs of Islam: Religion and Politics in Iran' in G. Makdisi (ed.) Arabic and Islamic Studies in Honor of Hamilton A.R. Gibb, Leiden
Browne, E.G. (1910) The Persian Revolution 1905-1909, Cambridge
Calmard, J. .'Ayatullah' Encyclopaedia of Islam (2nd. ed.)
Fischer, M. (1980) Iran: From Religious Dispute to Revolution, Cambridge, Mass. and London
Halliday, F. (1979) Iran: Dictatorship and Development, Harmondsworth

Keddie, N.R. (1972) 'The Roots of the Ulama's Power in
    Modern Iran' in idem., (ed.) Scholars, Saints and Sufis,
    Berkeley, Los Angeles, London
Idem., (1966) 'The Origins of the Religious-Radical Alliance in
    Iran', Past and Present, 34:70-80
Idem., (1980) Iran: Religion, politics, and society, London
Idem., (1981) Roots of Revolution. An Interpretive History of
    Modern Iran, New Haven
Idem., (1966) Religion and Rebellion in Iran; the tobacco
    protest of 1891-1892, London
Idem. and Zarrinkub, A.H. 'Fida'iyyan-i Islam',
    Encyclopaedia
    of Islam
Idem. and Bonine, M.E. (eds.) (1981) Modern Iran. The
    Dialectics of Continuity and Change, Albany, N.Y.
Khumaini, R. (1978) Vilayat-i faqih, Tehran
Lambton, A.K.S. (1964) 'A Reconsideration of the Position of
    the Marja^c al-Taqlid and the Religious Institution' Studia
    Islamica, 20:115-35
MacEoin, D.M. (1979) 'From Shaykhism to Babism: a study in
    charismatic renewal in Shi^ci Islam', unpublished Ph.D.
    dissertation, Cambridge
Idem., (forthcoming) 'Religious Heterodoxy in
    Nineteenth-century Iranian Politics', International Journal
    of Middle East Studies
Richard, Y. (1980) Le Shi^cisme en Iran. Imam et revolution,
    Paris

A MOVEMENT OF RENEWAL IN ISLAM

Derek Hopwood

On the morning of 20th November 1979, the routine of the pilgrimage in the Great Mosque of Mecca was interrupted by the announcement through a loud-speaker of the appearance of a new mahdi who had come to cleanse a corrupt Arabia. Hundreds of the mahdi's followers emerged from the crowd of worshippers to occupy the mosque. It took several days and many deaths for the Saudi authorities to regain control and to quell the movement.

In December 1980 perhaps as many as 8000 people were killed in Kano in Nigeria in a religious uprising. They were followers of a mahdi who had led them to the central mosque in an attempt to proclaim a new era of reformed Islam. These two events, widely separated geographically, had much in common. Two self-proclaimed mahdis had so convinced large numbers of men and women of their claims that they were ready to face impossible odds and almost certain death in the cause. Both leaders were protesting against the corrupt nature of the societies in which they lived and called for a return to an undefiled Islamic society. Both were declared heretics by the official ^culama; both chose significant Muslim dates on which to proclaim their uprising - in Mecca on the first day of the new century, in Kano on the Prophet's birthday. Both movements laid bare feelings of deep discontent with the path which society was following.

In October 1981 President Sadat of Egypt was assassinated by members of an Islamic group as punishment for having corrupted Egyptian society with false, non-Muslim values. Once again men were prepared to die for deeply held convictions born of almost complete desperation. Such feelings are not confined to one part of the Islamic world. They are widespread and constitute part of what may be termed an Islamic response to change forced upon societies unwilling to accept such change. What is happening in these societies? Can general statements be made about a series of such responses at different times and in different places? Can one look into the hearts and minds of men to discover what exactly has motivated them? Caution must be exercised in making general statements which may over-simplify the situation. There may be less uniformity than is at first thought. Is it possible to talk of an Islamic resurgence or revival? The terms used have to be chosen with care. A general assumption that Islam is experiencing a revival can be misleading in several ways. Revival implies the bringing to life of something that had been dead or at least moribund. Nothing could be further from the truth. Islam has been a permanent factor in the lives of believers for centuries but it has become obvious to the West only in recent years.

Secondly, the attention being paid at present to the activities of certain Muslims may suggest that these activities are new phenomena in the history of Islam. Such a suggestion ignores the fact that throughout Islamic history there has been a continuous series of such movements or activities, usually known as Jihads, that is a struggle against unbelievers, corruption or slackness in religious observation, or against foreign invaders, led by convinced activists who proclaimed that they alone were the sole guardians of the orthodox faith. As a basis for a reformed society they looked back to an ideal early Islam – a time when the shari^{c}a reigned supreme in a society untroubled by later heresies and innovations, when the Prophet guided believers' lives. These movements have ranged from those of the first Islamic century to the Wahhabis, the Sudanese Mahdists and those of the present century. The pattern of these movements has often been quite consciously based on the actions and experiences of the Prophet himself. The life of Muhammad can be very briefly classified as follows: he was born into a situation of disruption; he felt called to be a preacher and after inner struggle, retreat and crises he discovered his 'cause'; he then announced his message on the basis of his inspiration; he convinced a few followers but had to make his hijra; in Medina he was concerned to convert, train, discipline and inspire a new band of believers; they followed him in a Jihad against the unbelievers; with success he was able to found and organize a new community; he handed on his authority to designated but less charismatic lieutenants. This pattern has been repeated endlessly throughout Islamic history with certain personal and local variations. It has become the norm rather than the exception. Such movements have attempted to be restorative – Muslims would term them movements of tajdid (renewal) and the leaders mujaddidun – always attempting to bring the Islamic community back to the straight path, and, although frowned upon by the ^{c}ulama, they have been as responsible for the persistance of traditional Islam as those orthodox ^{c}ulama. Thirdly, the present concern with an Islamic resurgence may give the impression that there is currently a uniform process of renaissance throughout the Islamic world, that Muslims everywhere advance the same or similar formulae for the future of their world. On the contrary, there is no uniform prescription - apart from one in the most general terms - and there are many signs of divergence. One striking reason for this is that Islam is closely identified with the politics of nation states. It has never been divorced from politics; in fact the reform movements just mentioned all had as their aim the establishment of an ideal state in which the religious life could be lived without let or hindrance. No, it is the identification of Islam with nationalism which can cause dissension. Thus there is, or has been, war between Iraq and Iran, dispute between Syria and Jordan, Egyptian isolation, Libyan eccentricity, Saudi intrigue - all carrying religious overtones.

Current Islamic activity may seem to be something new because it is so obvious and has been thrust upon the consciousness of the rest of the world. Khumaini is the most widely known Islamic leader ever because of the attention of the media. Outsiders have for the first time heard the shouts of Allahu akbar and are told that America is the great evil in the world in a struggle against Islam. The fighters in Afghanistan are resisting the Soviet invader in the name of nationalism and Islam, calling themselves by the traditional name of mujahidin -- those who wage Jihad against the non-Muslim -- just as the Muslim leader Shamil did in the Caucasus against Tsarist invasion in the nineteenth century. This awareness of Islamic vitality has equally aroused in the West the centuries-old subconscious fear and mistrust of the Islamic world -- a fear deriving from the time of the Crusades and from the ever-present threat of the Ottoman Empire to conquer Christian Europe. Egyptian military manuals likewise write of the army having to wage a Jihad. In a manual of orientation in 1965, war against Israel was desribed as Jihad, as was the war in Yemen, a war against fellow Muslims who did not accept the revolutionary line! Jihad has therefore to be fought against Zionism, imperialism and Arab reaction. These ideas were repeated in the manuals of 1973 and it is significant that Sadat codenamed the 1973 crossing of the Suez Canal 'Badr' in memory of the Prophet's vital victory over his Meccan enemies. Nor is it surprising that President Saddam Husain of Iraq assumed the title 'Hero of the new Qadisiyya' - referring to the great Muslim Arab victory over the infidel Persians in 636.

Three case studies of individual countries may help to illumine certain aspects of contemporary Muslim concern. Under President Sadat there were interesting developments in the political aspects of Islam in Egypt. Sadat had called the Nasser era a period of materialism and unbelief and he professed himself to be a sincere, believing Muslim motivated in all his actions by love of his fellow men. He did not, however, follow consistently Islamic policies, although there were hesitant moves in that direction from time to time. In fact his approaches to the West and Israel aroused resentment amongst fundamentalist Islamic groups. To some extent he was caught in a dilemma. When he relied on aid from Saudi Arabia he felt under pressure to prove that Egypt was a strict Muslim country. There were proposals to ban alcohol, to punish apostasy by death, and to introduce Islamic criminal penalties, such as amputation of the hand for theft. Nothing was done in this direction, and most Egyptians would probably be opposed to such measures or, for example, to any regression in the progress achieved in women's equality. When Sadat was ostracised by the Arabs after Camp David he was relieved to some extent of pressure and was, in the pursuit of liberalization and equality, able to introduce measures which moved Egypt in a different direction, not towards a non-Muslim society, but towards a less rigid interpretation of Islam. Sadat made a distinction which is not valid in Islam - that of a separation between religion and politics. He said in 1979: 'Those who wish to practise Islam can go to the mosques, and those who wish to engage in politics may do so through legal institutions'. He was driven to this attitude by the series of developments whereby citizens had engaged in more and more extreme politics. He first encouraged Islamic movements as an ally against the leftist opposition and by so doing opened a Pandora's box which proved difficult to control. After 1967 the Muslim Brothers had resumed some of their activities, especially among students. Nasser had released some of the previously detained Ikhwan, and Sadat completed the process. Others returned from exile and by the late seventies their propaganda and recruitment had noticeably increased. At least one Cairo mosque was in 1980 openly filled to overflowing with Brothers praying, and at the end of Ramadan a large public square (outside the ex-royal palace) was covered with carpets on which thousands of Brothers prayed. The journal propagating their philosophy, al-Da^{c}wa, reappeared in 1976 after being banned since 1954. Sadat allowed them this freedom of 'religious' action while withholding political status. This was resented, and there were calls for recognition as a political party able to participate in elections. They did not, however, resort to the kind of violence for which they had been well known in earlier years. For this reason, perhaps, more extreme groups emerged.

The basic programme of the Ikhwan did not change. It deplored the moral deterioration in Eygpt and called for the introduction of thoroughgoing Islamic principles based entirely on the shari^{c}a. Only thus would Egypt avoid the dangers of corruption and contamination from the West. They criticized Sadat for opening the country to too much Western influence. They criticized the socialist economy of Nasser because it failed to introduce a society of equality and justice and denied people their liberty. Nationalized industries actually transferred ownership of plants to the government and not the people. Under Sadat they aimed for the abolition of left-wing parties, the banning of communism as an atheistic creed, and the purging of the government and bureaucracy. They opposed the accommodation with Israel, a country which had usurped Islamic territory and against which the Jihad must continue. They were deeply disturbed by Egypt's isolation from the Islamic Arab world. The Ikhwan were one of the earliest groups to formulate their ideas in this century on the ideal future of the Muslim world. Their founder, Hasan al-Banna stated the problem thus (writing, of course, during the British occupation of Egypt): 'Europeans have worked hard to spread the tide of materialism with its corrupting features and deadly germs, to overwhelm all the Islamic lands towards which their hands are outstretched'(1). The mission of the Ikhwan was: 'To free the Islamic fatherland from all domination - this is the natural right of every human being and is denied by an unjust oppressor; to create a free Islamic state, acting according to the precepts of Islam, applying its social regulations, proclaiming its sound principles and broadcasting its mission to all mankind'(2). How was this mission to be achieved? 'God has imposed the Jihad on every Muslim categorically and rigorously, from which there is no evasion. He has made the reward of martyrs a splendid one, and threatened backsliders with the most frightful punishment'.

Under Sadat the Ikhwan succeeded in recruiting new members, especially amongst students and middle classes. Their propaganda was carried out on university campuses by Islamic groups whose activities were most obvious. The struggle for influence among students caused the government some disquiet and the authorities kept a wary eye on them, since their activities could easily have slipped into the political sphere. Sadat was implacably opposed to universities becoming, as he said, 'arenas of political rowdiness'.

More damaging were the activities of more extreme groups, notably the group of Penitence and Withdrawal - Jama͑at al-takfir wa-al-hijra - the title implies those who accuse society of unbelief and therefore withdraw from it. This is the age-old Islamic custom, beginning with the Prophet Muhammad, of migrating away from a corrupt society. The group's existence had been known from 1973, and it was implicated in an alleged plot to overthrow the government. Its ideology was a total rejection of existing conditions and a call for a return to a state of pure Islam where only the shari͑a would be applied. The Sunna of the Prophet would be the supreme example. There would be an inevitable confrontation with the ruling elite, since they had not set an example and since society's problems stemmed from their non-observance of Islamic principles. The leader of a state had to be a good

Muslim who abided by the shari^ca; if he did not, he had to be removed. The members of Takfir despised the ^culama as corrupt hypocrites and opportunists who stood in the way of building a true Islamic order. The leader of the group was Ahmad Shukri Mustafa, a disillusioned former member of the Ikhwan, most of whose followers were young students and others who felt alienated by the pattern into which Egyptian society had fallen. The leader demanded total commitment from his followers, who became isolated from the wider world in their complete devotion to him and the group. A deep sense of group solidarity developed together with a willingness to pay any sacrifice necessary for the cause. The group had long term aims. Mustafa declared himself to be the mahdi who would found a new community to conquer the whole world.

In July 1977 the group shocked the public by kidnapping and then murdering an ex-government minister (a member of the ^culama) when its demands were not met. Bombings and killings occurred in Cairo and 400 members of the group were arrested and accused of trying to overthrow the regime. Five were executed for the minister's death and others sentenced to imprisonment. This did not weaken them but strengthened their belief, inspired by the example of Iran. The government faced with such Muslim extremism reacted by trying to divert public criticism and announcing the reintroduction of the traditional Islamic penalties of death for apostasy and adultery and the whipping of drunkards. This was a panicky over-reaction, which caused considerable public concern and the government soon announced that the law on apostasy at least would be shelved.

Other similar groups appeared in Egypt. In November 1979 over one hundred members of a group called Jihad were arrested and charged with forming an anti-government party. In January 1980 the same group carried out bomb attacks against churches in Alexandria. It and other bodies were accused of receiving arms and aid from foreign governments (mainly Libya) in order to carry out sabotage.

In the midst of this religious ferment Sadat forbade any political party from being formed by a religious sect, and at the same time he sought Islamic legitimacy for his policies. He used the Azhar Islamic University to support his detente with Israel, much as Nasser had used it at various times. In May 1979 the ^culama issued a ruling on the peace treaty, which showed that the tradition of religious leaders supporting state policy was very much alive. They said:

> Egypt is an Islamic country, and it is the duty of its guardian to ensure its protection. If he considers that the interest of the Muslims lies in being gentle towards their enemies, this is permissible because he is responsible in matters of peace and war.... and more

knowledgeable about the affairs of his subjects..... The existence of treaties between Muslims and their enemies is governed by clear regulations established by Islam..... The Azhar ^culama are of the opinion that the Egyptian-Israeli treaty was concluded within the context of Islamic judgement. It springs from a position of strength following the waging of the Jihad and the victory (of October 1973).(3)

The statement ended with an appeal (warning?) from the Qur'an to other Muslims to follow Egypt's lead 'lest ye lose heart and your power depart'. Perhaps as a reward, and certainly as a sop to Muslim feeling, Sadat's amended constitution approved by referendum made the shari^ca the main soucre of legislation in Egypt.

But he had so alienated Muslim fundamentalist opinion that they followed the traditional precedent of punishing the one they held responsible for the moral corruption. No remorse was shown by any who took part in the assassination. Their leader, Lieutenant Khalid al-Islambuli declared: 'I killed the pharoah. This is a religious cause'.

Egypt has had a history of a century and a half's contact with Europe and a tradition of liberal progressive Islamic thought. The background to Saudi Arabia is quite different. From the eighteenth century on, the country has had a strict Wahhabi framework of Islamic observance introduced by a reformer in the mould of those already described. Ibn ^cAbd al-Wahhab had seen Arabian society as corrupt where religious life had sunk to a low level. He was inspired to try to remedy this situation and, in alliance with the house of Saud, was largely successful. It is ironic that the protest of 1979 should have taken place in Saudi Arabia and deeply shocking that the holiest mosque in Islam should have been the scene of such an incident. The leader of the movement was Juhaiman Ibn Saif al-^cUtaiba. He had received a military training but became so disillusioned with the state of Saudi society that he abandoned all thoughts of a career in order to pursue his religious aims - the dismantling of the Saudi state and its replacement with an uncorrupted Islamic society. He recruited young people to his cause, often students of the shari^ca, disoriented and enraged by the pace of change in the country. He was later to proclaim his brother-in-law the expected mahdi, a wild and unrealistic move.

Juhaiman's philosophy was:

We are Muslims who wanted to study the shari^ca but we quickly understood that it could not be done in these schools and colleges where no-one dares criticize the government. We know that one day we will be strong enough to name among us a mahdi and we shall take refuge at his command in the Great Mosque where we will proclaim the beginning of the new Islamic state.(4)

Juhaiman believed that he would receive divine help in overcoming the unbelievers. It was a sad and pathetic uprising with almost no hope of success. It is the disillusionment and the convictions of those who were prepared to risk their lives that are important. They demonstrate how extreme was the despair they felt. The Saudi government was shaken by the siege and the movement was crushed by force but they really had no answer to the moral demands posed by Juhaiman. Perhaps Ibn ^cAbd al-Wahhab would have approved of his dissatisfaction if not of his actions.

In Nigeria in 1980 Muhammad Marwa proclaimed himself mahdi and gained a following among the young and dispossessed of Kano, often recent converts or immigrants. He offered them teaching and guidance and a feeling of belonging to an elite group in an alien society. He preached against materialism and ostentation and promised to purify corrupt religious practices. He proclaimed a Jihad and set out to capture the central mosque in Kano. He promised his followers entry into paradise if they were killed. The ^culama condemned him as a heretic who was observing non-Islamic practices. Muhammad and his followers marched on the mosque in December 1980 crying 'There is only one God. All the people of Kano are unbelievers'. They were met by gunfire from the police. Muhammad had said they were invulnerable and they charged with their spears against machine guns. Thousands were killed and Muhammad died of his wounds.

This further sad example perhaps harks back to the movement led by ^cUthman Dan Fodio in Nigeria in the nineteenth century. He then preached against the introduction of local customs into Islamic observance by the ruling Hausa tribes. He made a hijra in 1804, gathered together a group of followers and proclaimed a Jihad. He was able to defeat the Hausa but became disillusioned in victory and returned to a life of contemplation. He said of himself: 'I am not the mahdi but I am clothed in his robe. Every era has a mahdi. Like the wind heralding rain, I stand in relation to him'. Dan Fodio's message was: 'Islam has been flagrantly abused by corrupt rulers. We must return to the Golden Age'(5).

Three different countries provide evidence of a feeling of discontent in the Islamic world, a feeling deeply held by many, but not by the majority of the population. The Islamic revolution in Iran offers more evidence of this feeling on a wider scale and it is possible to maintain that Khumaini is the most successful example to date of a leader of a movement of reform and of protest against a very specific object of complaint. The Iranian Jihad continues, and it is still unclear how the hoped-for Islamic state will work in practice and in what sense purely Islamic policies can be followed. Khumaini's vision is similar to that of other Muslim leaders, yet rather imprecise and idealistic:

> My dear youth, take the Qur'an in one hand and the weapon in the other. The oppressed will triumph. They shall inherit the earth and shall govern by God's decree. The entire victory was achieved through the will of almighty God, through faith and self-sacrifice.(6)

The present current of Islamic feeling is very noticeably a reaction, especially amongst the young, to unbearable and rapid change, to the pressures of modern life against which they turn by longing for the tranquility of earlier periods; a reaction against the West which has disrupted traditional life and values, to which they respond by holding on to known and tested values; a reaction against the corruption and decadence of those who have succumbed to the temptations of wealth and the secular life. No one and no state is immune from criticism, as the Saudis - in the eyes of the West a bastion of Islam - found to their cost when the young men seized the mosque in Mecca in the name of uncorrupted Islam.

Islam, then, is the rock to which many believers cling in a world of bewildering change, thereby asserting their own values and their own personality in the face of alien influences and alien values. As one Egyptian woman anthropologist has written:

> Some of us are trying to go back to our roots and start again from there. And then, and only then, to admit into our culture some aspects of the West, be they technical, cultural or scientific, that do not conflict with our basic concepts of our culture or of ourselves(7).

Or in the words of Ahmad Shukri Mustafa, a cry from the heart the sentiment of which perhaps some people in the West might echo:

> I reject the Egyptian regime and the Egyptian reality in all its aspects because everything is in contradiction to the shari'a and belongs to heresy. Our ideas are based on the shari'a of which we are the lawful guardians. We reject everything that has to do with innovation and is related to so called modern progress. We demand a return to natural simplicity, because mechanized society has taken control of minds and souls and made heresy worse and has made people forget the essence of their being and their religious duties.(8)

A Movement of Renewal in Islam

NOTES

1. Al-Banna, H., Majmu^cat rasa'il (Beirut, 1965), p.220.
2. Ibid., p.225.
3. Afro-Asian Affairs, 76, p.8.
4. Middle East Research and Information Project, 91, p.4. New Year speech (abbrieviated).
5. Al-Masri, F.H. et al., 'Sifofin Shehu; an autobiography and character study of Uthman b. Fudi in verse', Centre of Arabic Documentation Research Bulletin, 2, 1966, p.11.
6. Middle East Research and Information Project, 88, p.22.
7. Listener, July 29, 1982.
8. Al-Anwar, July 31, 1977.

REFERENCES

Ayoob, M.(ed.)(1981) The Politics of Islamic Reassertion, Croom Helm, London
Al-Banna, H. (1965) Majmu^cat rasa'il, Beirut, trans. Wendell, C. (1978) Five tracts of Hasan al-Banna', University of California Press
Esposito, J.L.(ed.)(1980) Islam and Development; Religion and Sociopolitical Change, Syracuse University Press, N.Y.
Martin, B. (1976) Muslim Brotherhoods in 19th-century Africa, Cambridge University Press
Peters, R. (1979) Islam and Colonialism; the Doctrine of 'jihad' in Modern History, Mouton, the Hague

ISLAM AND ECONOMIC DEVELOPMENT(1)

Rodney Wilson

During the last three decades there has been increasing discussion of Islamic teaching on economics. Both the Qur'an and the Sunna have much to say on economic questions, as Muhammad himself recognised that spiritual concerns could not be divorced from everyday behaviour. Hence the Prophet specified a code of conduct for inter-personal relations, which involves economic laws as well as social strictures more generally. Islamic teaching in the economic sphere has relevance for all the fundamental issues in development, including saving, investment finance and capital accumulation, while it also deals specifically with income distribution through its laws on taxation and inheritance.

Much of the debate on Islamic economic doctrine in the 1950's and 1960's was largely concerned with how Qur'anic ideas could be reconciled with the practices of capitalism or socialism, although more often the latter than the former. In most of the Islamic world the political leaders had long been preoccupied with liberation from colonialism, and many saw this continuing as a struggle against economic exploitation through neo-colonialism even after political independence. Inevitably some sought to assert their independence by emphasizing the differences between Islam and the capitalistic economic practices of the West. Often however, the political leaderships were attracted by some of the socialistic ideas of the Eastern European states, whom many viewed as allies in the anti-imperialist struggle. There was a desire to synthesise Islamic teaching at least with socialism, if not with communism, although these efforts in the end proved relatively short lived.

The last decade has seen the abandonment of attempts to relate Islam to both capitalism and socialism in either a negative or positive fashion. Instead of trying to reconcile the laws and practice of Islam to these foreign and essentially materialistic ideologies, there has been a reassertion of traditional Islamic values. What has occurred is an attempt to make economic practice conform to these values, rather than any re-interpretation of basic doctrine. With the rejection of both capitalism and socialistic systems, there is no need to reformulate Islamic ideology, or to compromise its tenets. Such compromise was always anathema to the fundamentalists in any case. Instead an Islamic economic system is being proposed as a complete alternative to either a capitalistic or socialistic system. New institutions have been established such as the Islamic banks and development assistance agencies with the aim of translating Islamic ideals into practical solutions.

Before examining some of these solutions, it is instructive to contrast Islamic ideology with other ideologies. In particular it is useful to compare Islamic ideas with those of socialism, not least because this gives some indication as to why so many socialist experiments in the Islamic World have failed completely.

The introduction of Arab socialism into Nasser's Egypt as well as Ba^cthist Syria and Iraq represented perhaps the most far reaching attempt to impose a socialist ideology on Islamic states. Emphasis was placed on establishing strong centralised government, which would play a leading role in the economy. At first sight there appeared to be no conflict between this goal and the ideals of Islam. The Qur'an condemns disorder and anarchy, and praises order and organisation. The Prophet extorts Muslims to select a leader (an amir) even if three of them were travelling together(2). The leader is to be listened to and obeyed, as long as there is no conflict between his directions and Islamic law. The power of the ruler is not absolute however, as he must submit to the law of God himself, indeed his obedience should provide an example for his subjects.

Unfortunately few Arab socialist leaders managed to live up to these high standards and command the respect and obedience of the devout. In addition their attempts to secularise the legal system were resented, even though Islamic laws were maintained. Still more objectionable, however, was the overriding of property rights which seemed to be implicit in socialist economic policies. The nationalisation of businesses included many which believers either owned outright, or had a stake in. Sweeping land reforms resulted in expropriation of large areas of agricultural land, and the breakdown of the social order in the countryside. Admittedly the first land expropriated in countries such as Egypt was owned by foreigners or the former royal family, who were scarcely held in respect by devout Muslims. As the land reforms progressed, however, the farms of many devout landlords were taken away even in Egypt, while in Iraq and Syria it was the devout who saw themselves as penalised from the start.

Under Islamic law it is improper for a Muslim to acquire the property of someone without the owner's consent, and the state has no right to forcibly expropriate property(3). If the public interest necessitates it, a certain piece of property can be acquired from an individual, but compensation must be paid which would cover the owner for his loss. During the time of the Prophet there was considerable emphasis on public works programmes such as road building and the provision of water supplies. Property could be acquired for these purposes which were considered to be legitimately in the state domain. In general, however, there are few guidelines in Islamic law as to how far state control should extend. Nevertheless, there is a recognition that private individuals should not benefit merely from ownership as such without providing some service. The Prophet, for instance, gave Abyad ibn Hammal permission to mine salt at Maarib in the Hijaz, which looked at first sight the best way of exploiting this resource. When Muhammad was later advised how easy it was to extract the salt, he withdrew the franchise given to Hammal(4). The income Hammal was receiving was simply of a rentier nature, rather than because of any work which he had put into the mine.

For devout Muslims in the last analysis all wealth, including land, is owned by God. The human owner is merely seen as an agent trusted with the wealth, and he is accountable for the way he uses it. The rewards of property cannot be earned without the owner utilising his resources in a socially beneficial way. Property is not to be accumulated as an end in itself, but as a means of serving society as a whole. Not all individuals are equally endowed with resources, but personal ability also varies. For believers an uneven distribution of property can be justified in the interests of efficiency, as long as those with the greater property rights are aware of their obligations to the poorer members of society.

There are, however, two major checks on the accumulation of property, a wealth tax (zakat) and the inheritance laws. Under the Islamic inheritance system the will of the deceased is enforceable only on one third of his estate, and it is expected that if the individual exercises this limited discretionary right he should provide for those members of society who stand to gain least by inheritance themselves(5). Thus the individual's control over his property is much more limited than in most socialist, and even communist societies. For the remaining two thirds of the estate, or the whole estate if the individual does not exercise his discretionary powers, Islamic law provides for distribution according to a fixed formula. This decrees that all sons and daughters are entitled to a share in their parent's estate, with sons receiving twice as much as daughters. What a daughter inherits remains her own however, even after she marries, and there is no pooling of funds between the sexes as in western societies. A widow should inherit one quarter of her husband's estate on his death, the remainder going to the children unless the grandparents are alive, in which case they inherit one sixth of the estate each. If the wife dies first, the widower similarly inherits only one quarter of his wife's estate, the remainder going to the children unless the mother-in-law and father-in-law are alive(6). This formula ensures that substantial estates soon get dispersed, especially today given the large family sizes in most Muslim countries. Muslims disapprove completely of the system of primogeniture under which in some western countries the eldest son alone inherited the entire estate, and the other children were disinherited. Even in Islamic monarchies such as Saudi Arabia it is not necessarily the eldest son who succeeds to the throne. The successor must be approved by the entire family, and a son can be passed over if he is not deemed sufficiently competent. Muslims regard primogeniture as not only unfair, but inefficient. The eldest son may not be the most suitable person to manage an estate.

Weath taxes are rare in socialist countries, and none of the communists states of Eastern Europe levy taxes of this type. It is only in Social Democratic Sweden that a wealth tax is levied, and that country is often hailed as the most egalitarian in Europe, East or West. Yet according to Islamic law, a Muslim, as part of his religious obligation, has to contribute two and a half per cent of his net worth each year to the zakat or social security fund. This tax is collected by the state, as was the procedure in the days of the Prophet, but it is administered separately from other tax revenues. Hence it is not a substitute for other taxes, but a complement, which is to be used to help the poorest members of society. The application of the tax varies widely in the modern Muslim world, with Pakistan and Saudi Arabia going furthest in introducing it. In Saudi Arabia payment of the zakat is entirely voluntary, but most belivers pay, for 'whoever offers prayers but does not pay zakat, his prayers are in vain'(7).

Zakat is, of course, a proportionate rather than a progressive tax, and its rate is fairly modest. The Prophet himself urged wealthy believers to give alms in addition to their zakat payments, but the amounts were left to the conscience of the individual Muslim. The less affluent are also expected to pay zakat, but the proportionate nature of the tax means their financial burden is light. Nevertheless, payment of the tax increases their sense of solidarity with their fellow Muslims, and therefore it is believed it would be wrong for the less affluent to be deprived from contributing. Indeed, insofar as their sacrifice is greater than that made by the more wealthy, it is even more praiseworthy.

Investment and capital accumulation are recognised in most Islamic societies as being as essential for development as they are in both the western and communist worlds. Labour productivity, and hence wages, can only be raised if the capital intensity of production increases. Investment however is not stressed above all other priorities in an Islamic state. The development which investment can bring is welcomed as it makes possible improvements in the welfare level for the population as a whole. In Muslim societies, however, in periods of economic difficulty the poor are provided for through alms giving as well as through the zakat. Development will raise zakat revenues, but not necessarily alms giving, especially if it is achieved by the population becoming more individualistic and possibly more selfish. In these circumstances development will not improve the plight of the poor. It may be a mixed blessing as the material well-being of the richer members of the society is only improved at the expense of their spiritual well-being.

Investment has to be financed either through private savings, or else from tax revenue, which amounts to a form of compulsory savings. There are no specific guidelines about how great the burden of tax should be in Muslim states, and hence about how great a role state finance should play in investment. The means by which funds are invested have, however, been discussed extensively by Islamic scholars. In particular where finance is through lending, either directly or through a banking system, the Qur'anic prohibition of usury applies. Investors are not to derive their income from usury: 'Those that live on usury shall rise up before Allah like men whom Satan has demented by his touch; for they claim that usury is like trading. But Allah has permitted trading and forbidden usury'(8).

The unfavourable contrast of living on usury with trading activity makes it clear that usury is seen as unproductive, whereas trading is seen as a useful activity. The deferment of consumption is not to be encouraged, and certainly not rewarded for its own sake. Saving for old age, or to purchase a particular good, or to provide for future family needs, is of course legitimate. However, saving for capital accumulation as an end in itself is viewed as undesirable. If this results in consumption being reduced, markets may collapse, and a situation of Keynesian demand failure may occur, as most economists recognise(9). Another quotation from the Qur'an illustrates the objection to hoarding:

> Proclaim a woeful punishment to those that hoard up gold and silver and do not spend it in Allah's cause. The day will surely come when their treasures shall be heated in the fires of Hell, and their foreheads, sides and backs branded with them. Their tormentors will say to them 'These are the riches which you hoarded. Taste then the punishment which is your due'.(10)

Islam and Economic Development

One objection to interest is simply that it is a reward gained without productive effort. Western economists regard it as a reward for waiting, or postponing consumption. Goods consumed in the future are worth less today, and their value has to be discounted. This process of discounting introduces the interest element. For Muslims, as time is not money these western concepts cannot apply. Interest, however, is also viewed as objectionable because of its adverse redistributive effects. It makes the more productive indebted to the less productive, and can also result in the poor being indebted to the rich. Where a debtor gets into difficulty with repayments, the Qur'an urges leniency with debt rescheduling: 'If your debtor be in straights, grant him a delay until he can discharge his debt; but if you can waive the sum as alms it will be better for you if you but knew it'(11).

These Islamic strictures on usury are interpreted in different ways in the Islamic world today. One response has been the rise of Islamic banking.

Although these remain insignificant in aggregate terms, Islamic Banking institutions operate in most Gulf states, the Dubai Islamic Bank being the largest. The Islamic banking movement first started in Pakistan as far back as the 1950's, but spread to Egypt in the early 1960's. In Egypt its main strength was in the provincial towns of the delta rather than in Cairo or Alexandria, where the secular nationalised banks did most of their business. Today Islamic banking has even spread to Europe, with an international Islamic bank operating out of Geneva(12), which is controlled through a Cayman Islands based holding company.

Islamic banks do not pay their depositors interest, but rather they provide for profit sharing(13). It is perhaps useful to illustrate their operation with reference to the Dubai Islamic Bank, as this typifies the others. Two types of accounts are provided for depositors by the Dubai Islamic Bank: savings accounts and investment accounts. No interest is earned on savings accounts, but depositors qualify for interest free loans, and many depositors who have not made use of this loan facility nevertheless regard it as worthwhile to maintain funds in such an account as it offers them security. Those who open investment accounts are entitled to share in the profits from the bank's investments, but funds have to be maintained in such accounts for a certain minimum period to qualify, normally a year. Funds cannot be withdrawn from investment accounts on demand, as notice must be given in advance, but the bank is fairly flexible about this, and usually one month is the notice stipulated for small amounts, and three months for larger sums. If a client needs funds urgently and is in financial difficulties, the bank is always understanding, especially as it is aware of its religious obligations. Debtors will never be squeezed under any circumstances, the bank will instead offer advice about

124

how their financial affairs should be reorganised. Obviously the record and moral standing of the client is taken into account when help is offered, and this will play a part in determining the conditions attached to the help given.

Those who receive money from the bank for business purposes have to pay the bank a share of the profits of their businesses. The bank is really investing money rather than lending, and the bank is sharing the risks with the client. If there are no profits, the bank will not get a return on its investment. This means that sound investment appraisal is necessary before funds are advanced. A bank such as the Dubai Islamic Bank has to function as a merchant bank in assessing risk, although this fits in well with the merchant traditions of that part of the Gulf.

Another response to Islamic structures has been to allow conventional banks to operate, but to prohibit interest payments and receipts by law. This is the practice in Saudi Arabia, where banks levy service charges on borrowing, but do not charge interest(14). This is no matter of mere semantics. Interest is not permitted to be paid as a reward to those depositors who have time or savings accounts. Most deposits in Saudi Arabia in any case are in current accounts which earn no return. There is however a growing volume of savings accounts, especially with the former foreign- owned banks which were recently Saudi-ised(15). Returns are payable to compensate for inflation - in other words nominal interest is permitted, but not real interest - to compensate for deferring consumption. The distinction between nominal and real payments is seen as critical in Saudi Arabia. Similarly the service charges levied on borrowers are partly to cover the administrative overheads of the banks, but a margin is also allowed for inflation. The Banks should not charge their clients real interest, but neither should they subsidise their borrowers by charging zero nominal interest.

As all banks function according to Islamic principles and the shari‍ᶜa law in Saudi Arabia, there is no need for special Islamic banking institutions to serve believers. The only specifically Islamic financial institution is the Jeddah-based Islamic Development Bank, but it is an external development aid agency, and does not finance internal development in Saudi Arabia(16). The low returns on bank deposits in Saudi Arabia have, however, made many reluctant to deposit funds within the country. In the absence of controls on outward capital movements, many depositors have placed money overseas, especially given the high returns available in international financial markets. This has caused problems for the Saudi financial system, with borrowers often forced to go outside the Kingdom for loans which local banks are unable to supply. Hence, although funds could be borrowed in 1982 from the National Commercial Bank or the Riyadh Bank at eight per cent in line with inflation (zero real interest), many borrowed from the Bahrain offshore banks at fifteen per cent and more. Clearly this is a worry for the authorities.

One way of avoiding risks is by taking insurance cover which comes in many forms. In Islam, however, there are two objections to insurance, one fundamental, and one regarding the operation of insurance companies themselves. The fundamental objection concerns trying to cover against future events, which are seen to be the will of God. This fatalistic interpretation of Qur'anic teaching is mainly adhered to in Saudi Arabia where all insurance companies are prohibited from registering within the country. Foreign registered insurance companies give cover in the Kingdom, but there are no local Saudi Arabian insurance companies. There are, however, some foreign insurance companies under part Saudi ownership, mainly in the Far East.

The second objection concerning the way insurance companies operate, is to their asset holdings. Often insurance companies invest their clients' funds in long-term interest yielding securities. In Dubai, however, the Islamic Bank has established an insurance subsidiary, the Arab Islamic Insurance Company. This is organised as a kind of mutual society. Premium income is invested in accordance with shari'a principles, and a small cash reserve is held for contingencies. Participants agree to help other members by increasing their subscriptions if there are a large number of clients putting in claims at the same time, but they are reimbursed by the company eventually. Those receiving assistance are expected to repay at least some of the compensation they obtain, unlike the practice with conventional insurance companies. This last proviso is justified, partly in order to keep down premium levels, but also so that all participants feel a sense of solidarity with the others involved, in line with Islamic teaching. The identification and the commitment are with the other members rather than an impersonal corporate entity, and the emphasis is on mutual sharing.

There is no doubt that further new types of financial institutions will be developed to serve the Islamic world. Qur'anic principles, far from being a constraint, are being interpreted in an innovative fashion in the Gulf and elsewhere. This emphasis on the positive rather than the negative contrasts with the view of Islam sometimes held in western financial circles. Indeed it may well be that by studying the workings of the new Islamic institutions western financial specialists can gain a greater insight into the defects and merits of their own institutions.

Can much be learnt from the historical experience of Islamic societies about the effects of Islam on development? In the nineteenth century there was a tendency amongst European economists to equate Islam with backwardness, which was perhaps not surprising given the disintegrating state of the Ottoman Empire at that time. Today this disparaging view of the Islamic countries is much less prevalent, especially as the world's richest states in terms of per capita income, Kuwait and the United Arab Emirates, are Islamic. Of course per capita income is often an inadequate indicator of a country's level of development. Nevertheless anyone witnessing the rapid economic progress of Saudi Arabia under its second and third development plans must be impressed. There can be little doubt that the state that is the guardian of Islam's holiest places is also deeply committed to development. Furthermore, during the first two centuries after the Prophet's death, the rapid spread of Islam westward from Arabia as far as the Atlantic, and eastward to the Indian sub-continent and beyond, illustrates the dynamism of Muslim believers. The transformation of these societies during this period would suggest that the adoption of Islam aids rather than hinders development.

Another frequently voiced criticism of Islamic societies is that although they excel in the field of trading, their success in manufacturing activity has been more limited. It is certainly the case that the Prophet himself extolled the virtues of trading activity, contrasting it favourably with the practice of living off usury as has already been seen. Mecca and Medina were great centres of trade and exchange during the life of Muhammad, and the bazaars and souks of the Islamic world have long been renowned. Trading is seen as a useful and productive activity, and those that engage in it should be rewarded for the service they provide. However, the bazaars and souks often contained as many craftsmen as traders, and the distinction between handicrafts, industry, and trade was not always easy to draw. Skilled artisans were equally praised by the Prophet for their toils, and the craft traditions of the Islamic world surpassed those of most Western countries. In the sixteenth century for instance, Isfahan, the capital of the Safavid dynasty, had more skilled artisans than Paris, then the West's largest city.

Islam does not emphasise material incentive, since physical rewards are seen as a means rather than an end in themselves. Muslims entrusted with material resources have a duty to God to see that they are not abused. Believers are urged 'to enjoy the bounties provided by God'(17), and no quantitative limits are set on the extent of material well-being, Muslims should make the most of the resources at their disposal, indeed they should strive to gain mastery of nature. According to the Qur'an, all the earth's resources have been created for the service of mankind. Only alcohol and unclean meat are prohibited, as these would dull the senses, either directly or through illness, thus preventing believers making the most of their own potential. Apart from these prohibitions there is no stress on abstinence from other types of consumption. Islam is designed to serve as a blessing for mankind, and aims at making life richer and worth living rather than poorer and full of hardship. Muslims are urged to work for their living and to refrain from begging: 'The best income is that earned honestly by the hard-working labourer .... When a wearied labourer returns home after sedulously working in an honestly-earned livelihood in the evening, he is forgiven his sins'(18). Hard work and spiritual fulfillment are equated, indeed work is seen as a duty. Workers are to be treated with dignity, and the empolyee-employer relationship is to be based on mutual respect, especially when they are part of the same Islamic brotherhood. Employers should ensure that workers are paid enough to satisfy their basic needs according to the Qur'an, and this has been taken as a justification for minimum wage legislation in some Islamic states. Workers should be paid promptly, and the conditions of work set by legal contract. Islam does not go beyond these basic conditions, and no criteria are specified for the determination of wages. Rewards based on skill and productivity are permissable, but the main aim of the system of remuneration should be to ensure that the worker can identify with the enterprise. Hence profit sharing schemes are encouraged(19). Islam favours working proprietors in close touch with their workforces rather than impersonal investment companies directly controlling labour.

It is probably misleading to speak of a complete Islamic economic system which can be presented as an alternative to capitalism or socialism. In recent years, nevertheless, some Islamic scholars have attempted to do exactly that, as already indicated. The problem is that it is not easy to identify a specifically capitalist or socialist economic system in any case, as there are so many variations between nations, and within nations over time. This is also the case in the Islamic world given the heterogeneity of Muslim states in terms of environment and peoples(20). Nevertheless, Islam provides a range of fixed rules which can be applied in all these diverse societies. It does not give a detailed masterplan for development, Muslims themselves are supposed to show initiative. What the Qur'an attempts is to define the conditions under which economic relations between individuals, families and states can be conducted. The objective is to ensure that spiritual and material aspirations and needs are reconciled. The believer will find this task difficult, and as the history of the Islamic World shows, few states have managed to implement effectively the strictures of the Qur'an and Sunna. Nevertheless the Muslims must try to live up to Islamic ideals; the effort itself is a blessed duty.

NOTES

1. An earlier version of this paper was presented to the British Society for Middle Eastern Studies (BRISMES)

Conference at Lancaster University in July 1982. A much shorter version based on this earlier presentation will appear in BRISMES Bulletin, 10, 1, 1983.
2. M. Umar Chapra, 'The Economic System of Islam: Part 4, Role of the State', The Islamic Quarterly, 14, 4 (October 1970), p.237.
3. Muhammad Abdul-Rauf, The Islamic Doctrine of Economics and Contemporary Economic Thought (American Enterprise Institute, Washington, 1979), p.19.
4. Chapra, 'Role of the State', p.245.
5. Inheritance issues are discussed by Alfred Guillaume, Islam (Harmondsworth, 1954), p.179 ff.
6. M. Umar Chapra, 'The Economic System of Islam : Part 3, Spiritual Values and the Islamic Economic System', The Islamic Quarterly, 14, 3 (July 1970), p.153. A fuller account of the operation of the Zakat is given in S.A. Siddiqi, Public Finance in Islam (Ashraf Press, Lahore, 1948), pp.8-63.
7. The Koran, trans. by N.J. Dawood (Harmondsworth, 1956), pp.355-356.
8. The Koran, p.352.
9. Although it is argued that Keynesian economics as a whole is not applicable in Islamic societies because of the role of interest in the system. See M.M. Metwally, 'General Equilibrium and Macroeconomic Policies in Islamic Economies', L'Egypte Contemporaine, 70, No.378 (October 1979), pp.53-95.
10. The Koran, p.314.
11. Ibid., p.353.
12. Known as Dar al-Mal al-Islami (DMI), the House of Islamic Funds.
13. For a discussion of Islamic banking see Ingo Karsten, 'Islam and Financial Intermediation', International Monetary Fund Staff Papers, 29, 1 (March 1982), pp.108-142. Mohammad Mohsin, 'Feasibility of Commercial Banking Without a Rate of Interest and its Economic Significance', The Islamic Quarterly, 22, 4 (December 1978), pp.149-157. Abraham L. Udovitch, 'Bankers without Banks: Commerce, Banking and Society in the Islamic World of the Middle Ages' in Centre for Medieval and Renaissance Studies, UCLA, The Dawn of Modern Banking (Yale University Press, New Haven, 1979), pp.255-273. B.A. Bashir, 'Successful Development of the Islamic Banking System', paper presented to the conference of the British Society for Middle Eastern Studies, Lancaster University, July 1982.
14. For a detailed critique of the Qur'anic position on interest see Fazlur Rahman, 'Riba and Interest', Islamic Studies, 3, (1964), pp.1-43. Ziauddin Ahmad, 'The Quaranic Theory of Riba', The Islamic Quarterly, 22, 1 and 2 (January and June 1978), pp.3-14.
15. Under majority Saudi private ownership.

Indigenisation is distinct from nationalisation which would imply state ownership. See Rodney Wilson, 'The Evolution of the Saudi Banking System and its Relationship with Bahrain', in T. Niblock (ed.) State, Society and Economy in Saudi Arabia (Croon Helm, London, 1981), pp.278-300.

16. A critique of this bank is provided in Rodney Wilson, Banking and Finance in the Arab Middle East (forthcoming), chapter 4.

17. M. Umar Chapra, 'The Economic System of Islam : Part 1, Introduction', The Islamic Quarterly, 14, 1 (January 1970), p.5.

18. Hakim Mohammed Said, The Employer and the Employee - Islamic Concept (Dar Al-Fikr Al-Ilami, Karachi, 1972), pp.27-28.

19. Ibid., p.68.

20. G.Destanne de Bernis, 'Islam et Developpement Economique', Cahiers de L'Institut de Science Economique Appliquee, 106 (October 1960), p.135 ff. Some conclude from historical experience that Islam has little impact on economic life in any case, See Maxime Rodinson, Islam and Capitalism (Harmondsworth, 1974), p.185 ff.

REFERENCES

Ahmad, Ziauddin (1978) 'The Quaranic Theory of Riba', The Islamic Quarterly, 22, Nos. 1 and 2

Abdul-Rauf, Mohammad (1979) The Islamic Doctrine of Economics and Contemporary Economic Thought, American Enterprise Institute, Washington

Chapra, Umar M. (1970) 'The Economic System of Islam - a discussion of its goals and nature': Part 1 'Introduction'; Part 2 'Nature of the Economic System of Islam'; Part 3 'Spiritual Values and the Islamic Economic System', Part 4 'Role of the State', The Islamic Quarterly, 14, No. 1, pp.3-18; No.2, pp.91-96; No. 3, pp.143-156; No. 4, pp.237-251

Dawood, N.J. (1956) trans., The Koran, Harmondsworth

Destanne de Bernis, G. (1960) 'Islam et Developpement Economique', Cahiers de L'Institut de Science Economique Appliquee, 106, pp.105-146

Fazlur Rahman (1964) 'Riba and Interest', Islamic Studies, 3, pp. 1-43

Guillaume, Alfred (1954) Islam, Harmondsworth

Karsten, Ingo (1982) 'Islam and Financial Intermediation', International Monetary Fund Staff Papers, 29, 1, pp.108-142

Metwally, M.M. (1979) 'General Equilibrium and Macroeconomic Policies in Islamic Economies', L'Egypte Contemporaine, 70, No.378, pp.53-95

Mohsin, Mohammad (1978) 'Feasibility of Commercial Banking Without a Rate of Interest and its Economic

Significance', The Islamic Quarterly, 22, 4, pp.149-157
Niblock, T. (ed.) (1981) State, Society and Economy in Saudi
    Arabia, Croom Helm, London
Rodinson, Maxime (1974) Islam and Capitalism, Harmondsworth
Said, Hakim Mohammed (1972) The Employer and the Employee
    - Islamic Concept, Dar Al-Fikr Al-Ilami, Karachi
Siddiqi, S.A. (1948) Public Finance in Islam, Ashraf Press,
    Lahore
Udovitch, Abraham L. (1979) 'Commerce, Banking and Society
    in the Islamic World of the Middle Ages' in Centre for
    Medieval and Renaissance Studies, UCLA, The Dawn of
    Modern Banking, Yale University Press, New Haven,
    pp.255-273
Wilson, Rodney (1983) Banking and Finance in the Arab
    Middle East, Macmillan, London (forthcoming)

ARCHITECTURE IN THE ISLAMIC WORLD

Miles Danby

In this paper architecture is used in its widest sense to cover the built environment as a whole and not only the selected buildings generally acknowledged to be outstanding masterpieces of their time. If it can be accepted, as I believe it should, that architecture is the physical manifestation of social, cultural and economic forces, then architecture in the Islamic world forms a man-made setting to a way of life that is a traditional integration of religious values with social and economic customs.

There are now approximately 400 million Muslims distributed from Mauretania to Indonesia in one direction and from Mongolia to Malagasy in the other, embracing a wide range of cultures and climatic conditions. There is also an extreme variation in the economic and political systems affecting the everyday life of Muslims, ranging from those countries where Islamic principles form the very basis of government to others where Muslims must live through an everyday compromise with governments with alien policies and intentions, whether Christian, Hindu, Jewish, capitalist or communist.

Obviously, the central and pivotal building of Islam is the Ka^{c}ba. According to Burckhardt(1), it represents the cube, a crystalline synthesis of the whole of space which has each of its six faces in a primary direction: zenith, nadir and the four cardinal points. Predating Islam, it was rebuilt in 608 A.D. by the Quraysh when Muhammad was thirty five, and was formed of thirty one alternating courses of stone and wood covered in stucco(2). Placed in its sanctuary in the holy city of Mecca, it is traditionally covered with a black cloth with gold lettering (kiswa) which is changed annually. It forms the centre of the circumambulations which every pilgrim must perform during the Hajj. Its geographical position must be known to all Muslims wherever they are, since all prayers must be made facing Mecca and it is this direction, qibla, which governs the orientation of every mosque. The qibla is given physical form by the mihrab, a

niche built into the wall of the mosque which faces Mecca.
After the Ka^cba, the next most important building in
Islam is the Dome of the Rock of Jerusalem. As its name
implies, it is built over the rock whence tradition believes
Muhammad ascended on his night journey to heaven. Its
builder, ^cAbd al-Malik, intended the rock to be a place of
pilgrimage and to rival the church of the Holy Sepulchre in
magnificence. There is a large wooden dome supported on
four piers and twelve columns which are enclosed by an
octagonal wall forming two concentric ambulatories. The
interior is lined with marble and beautiful mosaics, while the
dome has two shells, the outer being encased with sheets of
lead and finished with gleaming plates of copper or brass
gilt. Like the Ka^cba it is non-directional in form and the
dome over a square or octagon forms the prototype for many
tombs of holy men and prominent personages in the Islamic
world, of which the Taj Mahal at Agra is probably the best
known to westerners.

The mosque or masjid (place of prostration) on the other
hand is, as already mentioned, uni-directional towards Mecca.
All mosques share this characteristic but vary considerably in
architectural form. The Great Mosque at Cordova in Spain
which was built in 705 A.D. by ^cAbd al-Rahman I of the
Umayyad dynasty from Damascus, originally had eleven aisles
formed by ten arcades at right angles to the qibla wall in one
vast rectangular space punctuated by a forest of columns
supporting the double row of arches under a plain ceiling.
There are direct openings to an open courtyard which is in
turn surrounded by high and heavy walls and was intended
for extended congregations on feast days. This single space
with the repetitive and equidistant columns expresses in
architectural terms the egalitarian philosophy of Islam, where
there is no hierarchy but only a shared faith and the
communion of all true believers.

A similarly noble effect was achieved by Ibn Tulun, the
Governor of Egypt, when he built his famous mosque in Cairo
during the period 876 to 879 A.D. The main covered space
continues into the open courtyard (sahn) without interrupting
doors to allow a huge congregation to act as a unity in
prayer outside and inside. It differs from the Great Mosque
at Cordova in that there are five arcades supporting the main
roof which are parallel to the qibla wall. These arcades also
differ in that there is only a single row of pointed arches
supported on large brick piers of majestic proportions coated
with fine stucco. The other three sides of the courtyard have
double arcades of similar size and proportion, while in the
centre stands a stone pavilion over a fountain which one
might assume was intended for ablutions before prayer. Ibn
Duqmaq, however, assures us that Ibn Tulun intended the
ablutions to be made at the back of the mosque on the
north-west side. There is yet another surrounding wall

outside the main structure to enclose both the ablutions and the minaret, which stands at the opposite end to the qibla wall.
The origin of the minaret dates from the time of Muhammad when he ordered Bilal to give the vocal call to prayer(3) from the highest roof in the neighbourhood, in contrast to the horn or shofar of the Jews and .the clapper used by the Christians, who later adopted bells for the same purpose. The minaret of Ibn Tulun's mosque has a complicated form. The lowest storey is square in plan with a staircase on the outside which made one complete turn. Above this is another storey which is circular in plan, again with an outside staircase which makes a little more than half a turn. This is surmounted by a small octagonal kiosk of two storeys. The three basic plan shapes of the square, the circle and the octagon are thus used in this minaret. The practical purpose of the minaret was gradually augmented with the symbolic purpose of indicating the vertical and transcendental dimension of man's otherwise two-dimensional existence. Minarets became taller, and with this came a greater emphasis on verticality culminating in the elegance of the Ottoman cylindrical minarets exemplified by the four of the Suleyman mosque at Istanbul. This type of minaret coupled with the sound of the call to prayer symbolised the magic of Islam to all non-Muslim visitors to Islamic countries. The positioning of the minaret and Friday mosque became the primary decision in urban planning to ensure its maximum visibility from the network of narrow streets which characterised the closely packed business and residential districts of Islamic cities and towns.
The functional purpose of the minaret has now been superseded by the use of the electric loudspeaker for the call to prayer, and now when a minaret is built with a new mosque it is a response to the need for a physical symbol. Indeed, the combination of dome and minaret is still considered to be a very powerful architectural statement of Islam in most Muslim countries, although there are many mosques to be found without either. The architectural form of the mosque follows one of the universal themes in the Islam - unity in diversity. The unity exists in the orientation, simplicity, plan and arrangement of space, the need for water for ablutions and central position in the community, whereas the diversity is found in the variation of constructional systems and local materials and their effect on form.
Although today mosques throughout the Islamic world follow the simple plan arrangement after the early examples already described, the three-dimensional form varies considerably according to the roofing and construction methods used, which are in turn affected by the choice of building materials. In Mali, Niger, northern Nigeria and Northern Ghana, there is a tradition of mosque building with

mud and timber which produces its own characteristic local architectural expression. One of the largest of these mosques is at Mopti in Mali. The main enclosed space has a flat roof supported by a large number of regularly spaced mud piers, while externally the vertical piers are expressed in a curved plastic manner appropriate to mud construction. The whole structure is tied together with horizontal timbers, some of which project out through the walls at regular intervals, which gives an interesting pattern accentuated by their shadows. These projecting timbers also serve a practical purpose in that they provide permanent scaffolding for the essential regular maintenance needed to preserve such construction.

In Bangladesh, on the other hand, the dome is frequently used in the design of mosques and has almost come to symbolise the mosque itself. There are cases of village mosques which have been built with a simple flat roof but have been provided with small solid vestigial domes at each corner of the roof, presumably to indicate that the building is a mosque.

Most of the states that originally embraced Islam combined both religion and state in the person of the ruler, who was responsible for all prominent buildings whether directly religious in function or not. Some of the rulers built palaces for their own use, and probably the most famous of these is the Alhambra at Granada in Southern Spain which dates from 1309-54. The buildings that remain today formed part of a larger development which probably continued the existing closely related series of courtyards, halls, fountains and gardens. The Islamic tradition which prohibited the representation of the human form grew up towards the end of the 8th century A.D., and together with the great contemporary contribution of the Arabs to the sciences, particularly geometry and mathematics, probably accounts for the great skills in surface decoration that were developed in the Islamic world.

The Alhambra demonstrates these skills to perfection, in that the decoration arises naturally from the construction and the constructional principle is often extended to the ornamentation of the surface in great detail. It was this principle that so excited the British architect Owen Jones in 1851 that he reproduced the 'Court of Lions' to two-thirds scale at the Great Exhibition in Hyde Park in London. In a lecture at Marlborough House the following year, he developed his proposition IV stating that 'Construction should be decorated. Decoration should never be purposely constructed'. Geometry forms the basis for much of the decoration, which is developed in a very sophisticated way from the circle, square, hexagon and octagon. Another source is the Qur'an itself, quotations from which are employed in the form of bands of calligraphy which are integral parts of the overall design of the interiors. Much of the decoration is moulded or covered in gypsum plaster which is sometimes painted or gilded.

The capitals of the marble columns and the arches are elaborately carved, and many arched openings in the throne room are finished with a series of highly intricate interlocking stalactites surmounted with incised arabesque decoration based on plant forms. The lower parts of the wall surfaces are covered with multi-coloured glazed tiles of varying size and shape and assembled in patterns with an elaborate geometric basis. The whole gives an overall impression of splendour which is obtained without any overbearing effects of superhuman scale. Balconies with richly patterned pierced marble windows overlook the town below, while arcades open directly to the courtyards with fountains and gardens.

Gardens, of course, represent Paradise, which in the Qur'an is described as having four gardens of the Soul, the Heart, the Spriit and the Essence, and should contain three essential components, a fountain, flowing water and fruit trees. The importance of water is again stressed, this time an element of repose achieved through psychological means. The presence of water enables cooling by evaporation to take place, which is essential in climates that are both hot and dry, while the gentle sounds of falling water produce psychological calm.

Islamic domestic architecture developed from house forms that existed prior to Islam. The courtyard house, for example, is generally considered to be typically Islamic but it existed in Pharaonic times and was used by the Greeks and Romans. It is true, however, that most traditional Islamic house plans are of the courtyard type, but it would seem that this form was retained because it did not conflict with the needs of Islam. Indeed, it is a plan form that can easily be adapted to maintain the degree of privacy required by the Islamic way of life. It is a tradition among Islamic peoples that male visitors to the home do not enter the family zone or meet the ladies of the household. This combined with the Islamic tradition of hospitality means that frequent visiting imposes a certain discipline in the arrangement of interior spaces. A guest room for the reception of male visitors, sometimes with its own entrance vestibule and washing facilities separate from, but with access to, the family zone, is a common requirement.

The traditional courtyard house to be found in Old Cairo (Bait al-Sihaimi is an example) meets this requirement with a series of reception spaces including a hall which rises two storeys high with pierced screens, permitting observation from the family apartments, which are confined to the first floor. A simpler arrangement is possible for smaller houses, with one room reserved for the reception of male guests, which may well be used by all members of the family when male visitors are not present. Sometimes the house is so planned as to form two courtyards with one for the use of family only and the other as the entrance courtyard used for the reception of guests. As can be seen, the emphasis is on privacy with the resultant inward-looking architectural expression of this need.

In Old Cairo, the only outward expression of the house is the entrance doorway at ground floor level with some restrained decoration on a simple archway in a plain stone surface. The design of the entrance is therefore a very important consideration and resulted in the tradition of elaborately carved doors set in comparatively simple openings to be found in the Middle East and the East African coast, where the doorways of Zanzibar and Lamu(4) are renowned for their richness and skilled craftsmanship. Although the courtyard form of house is common in Islamic countries it is used for reasons of precedent, convenience and climate, rather than being a necessary outcome of the Islamic need for privacy.

In fact, the traditional urban house types recorded in Suakin in the Red Sea by J.P. Greenlaw(5) are not arranged round a courtyard but are closely packed three-storey dwellings built of coral stone and timber with all openings on to the street. The top floor usually has an enclosed area open to the sky accessible to the adjoining rooms of the family. Through ventilation is achieved by the use of balcony windows with pierced timber screens of great delicacy and beauty known as rawashin, which are placed wherever possible in the external walls. The screens are framed to support panels of inter-locking elaborately turned timber rods placed close enough together to prevent the ingress of direct solar rays but at the same time allowing free circulation of air after the same principle of the pierced marble windows of the Alhambra and the jalis used in those parts of Asia ruled by the Moghuls. Similar screens known as mashrabiyya were used in Old Cairo, often in conjunction with decorative coloured glass panels at the top of a large containing timber frame, which gave a beautiful and subtle quality of light to the interior.

Indeed it was the beauty of the interiors of the houses in Cairo as well as the lively and colourful street scene that so intrigued the English nineteenth-century painter John Frederick Lewis that he lived there for ten years recording scenes of the urban life. He followed E.W. Lane, who also lived there from 1825 onwards recording Cairo life with words and drawings(6). But perhaps the most beautiful record of traditional Arab interiors in use is the collected sketch boards of the French painter Delacroix who made a great number of fresh and vivid watercolour sketches on his travels to Morocco in the 1830's.

This renewed interest in the Islamic world that occured

in Europe during the nineteenth century was set off by the invasion of Egypt by Napoleon in 1798. Napoleon took with him engineers and archaeologists who prepared detailed descriptions of what they found there, and the later publication of these thorough investigations started a fashion amongst intellectuals and artists for travel to the Middle East. However, the most far reaching effect of the interaction between Europe and the Middle East that followed Napoleon's invasion and subsequent colonialism was the pervasive westernisation of ideas and values which increased apace after the opening of the Suez canal.

The more recent discovery of oil in the Gulf and Iran in large quantities brought rapid wealth to these areas and increased the process of westernisation through the increased reliance on high technology and its associated dependence on high energy consumption. The general persistence of western technology throughout the Islamic world -- at first the railway, large scale civil engineering, and the steamer followed by the internal combustion engine, electrification, the aeroplane and radio -- is now further reinforced by the spread of electronic information and the flood of instant entertainment based on western materialistic values. These influences cause confusion and dismay as they increasingly conflict with the traditional value system of Islam. The built environment, of course, has reflected this contradiction in values and the social reaction to it. The adoption of building bye-laws based on foreign principles related to prevention of fire made the mashrabiyya illegal in new buildings in Cairo in the middle of the 19th century.

Step by step, the traditional interior changed as French and Italian Baroque styles were adopted for the new villas built by the rich merchant classes. The relatively simple but beautiful interiors relying on carpets, cushions and low tables carved and decorated in the traditional manner were supplemented by imitations of foreign examples with all the paraphernalia of chairs, tables, framed pictures, cupboards and other possessions to indicate wealth in the western manner.

The coming of the motor car, bus and lorry has completely changed the pattern of urban development. The traditional pattern of streets was based on pedestrian and animal traffic and a strict hierarchy of functions, although the principles are not immediately obvious to visitors since this pattern did not depend on the use of surveyors' straight lines and easily defined plots of land. On the contrary, it is a highly complex and compact network starting from the unit cell of the individual house with a group of close neighbours which are reached through a short passageway froming a semi-private space with no through access and often provided with its own gateway. Another secondary street gives access to a series of these residential quarters, and a number of these secondary streets would feed into a long main street dedicated predominantly to commercial activities, with religious and public buildings placed at strategic points having direct access to large public spaces. There is, therefore, a progression from completely private space to completely public space. The streets and passageways were kept to the minimum possible to maintain circulation, thus enabling the highest density to be achieved as well as allowing the streets to be shaded by the buildings during the mornings and afternoons when they were mostly used.

The introduction of the motor car has created the need for wider streets at the same time as ever increasing urbanisation has swollen the population of the cities. This has meant the deterioration of the traditional quarters as it became difficult to absorb motor traffic without noise and pollution and congestion. In many cities, wide avenues were cut through to relieve traffic congestion destroying the human scale of the cellular structure of the old areas, whereas in others these quarters were neglected and eventually cleared to make way for modern development. The new buildings were usually very different in concept and scale to those they replaced. The new development followed the pattern of the highly industrialised nations, tall monolithic buildings in the city centres where land values had increased, and single blocks set in the centre of a building plot in the suburbs which were extending the area of the cities at an increasing pace. These new buildings were outward looking in character, facing onto wide streets which were exposed to solar radiation and uncomfortable for pedestrians. Many now live in flats planned in the western style which make little or no allowance for the specific Islamic need for private and semi-private space.

The widespread use of reinforced concrete wall panels or thin brick outside walls means that the heat absorbed from solar radiation is stored and quickly passed to the interior which soon becomes overheated unless air conditioning in some form is used. The traditional expertise of designing buildings which interacted in a passive manner with the external climate to produce a comfortable interior climate has largely been lost. Most houses and flats are now designed from the points of view of economy and structural stability and occasionally an impressive external appearance is also an important consideration. It is usually taken for granted that any cooling or other climatic modification should be achieved through the use of expensive mechanical services in spite of the increasing costs of energy. Even in the oil-exporting states the costs of the use of modern buildings have risen sharply and have become an important financial consideration.

Fortunately, there has recently been a strong revival of interest in the problem of creating new buildings with an Islamic character. An important international symposium on

Islamic Architecture and Urbanism was held in 1980 at King Faisal University, Dammam, Saudi Arabia(7) which was attended by many architects and planners from Islamic countries as well as a number with a special interest in Islam from other countries. A declaration was made that this great architectural heritage of Islam is seriously endangered and stands at the threshold of irreparable loss. To prevent further deterioration of its natural environment the establishment of a central place for documentation, liaison and research was proposed, the main purpose of which is to disseminate those essential attitudes that can help nurture the Islamic way of life and the realisation of the appropriate architecture of Islam.

To conclude, the two main tasks for Islamic decision-makers and their architects today are, firstly, to promote the conservation of the historic architectural monuments and the remaining traditional commercial and residential districts, many of which are now under threat; secondly, to encourage the development of an architecture that expresses the spirit and thinking of the Islamic way of life in three-dimensional physical terms, which would not accept the application of 'Islamic arches' or similar devices to buildings fundamentally conceived according to western materialistic principles.

NOTES

1. Titus Burckhardt, Art of Islam (World of Islam Festival Publishing Co. Ltd., 1976), p. 4.
2. It was later rebuilt in 684 A.D. with walls of stone by Ibn al-Zubayr see K.A.C. Creswell, A Short Account of Early Muslim Architecture (Harmondsworth, 1958), pp. 1-4 and p. 15.
3. Ibid., p.5.
4. Usam Ghaidan, Lamu, a Study in Conservation (East African Literature Bureau, Nairobi, 1976), p. 21.
5. Jean-Pierre Greenlaw, The Coral Buildings of Suakin (Oriel Press, Stocksfield, 1976).
6. Edward William Lane, Manners and Customs of the Modern Egyptians (reprint of 1895 edition by East-West Publications, The Hauge and London, 1978).
7. See Ekistics volume 47 number 280 (Athens, January/February 1980). This number was entirely devoted to Islamic human settlements and contains extracts from many of the papers presented at this symposium which discuss most of the issues described in this paper.

REFERENCES

Burchhardt, T. (1976) Art of Islam, World of Islam Festival Publishing Co. Ltd.

Architecture in the Islamic World

Creswell, K.A.C. (1958) A Short Account of Early Muslim Architecture, Harmondsworth
Ghaidan, Usam (1976) Lamu, a Study in Conservation, East African Literature Bureau, Nairobi
Greenlaw, Jean-Pierre (1976) The Coral Buildings of Suakin, Oriel Press, Stocksfield
Lane, E.W. (1978) Manners and Customs of the Modern Egyptians, repr. of 1895 ed., East-West Publications, The Hague and London

Professor William M. Watt,
Professor Emeritus of Arabic and Islamic Studies,
University of Edinburgh

Professor Bryan S. Turner,
Professor of Sociology, Department of Sociology,
Flinders University of South Australia

Professor John F.A. Sawyer,
Professor of Old Testament Language and Literature,
Department of Religious Studies,
University of Newcastle Upon Tyne

Dr. Ralph W.J. Austin,
Senior Lecturer in Arabic,
School of Oriental Studies,
University of Durham

Professor Laurence P. Elwell-Sutton,
Professor Emeritus of Persian,
University of Edinburgh

Dr. Ahmed S. Al-Shahi,
Lecturer In Social Anthropology,
Department of Social Studies,
University of Newcastle Upon Tyne

Mr. John D. Norton
Lecturer of Turkish Studies,
School of Oriental Studies,
Director of the Centre for Middle Eastern and Islamic Studies,
University of Durham

List of Contributors

Dr. Denis M. MacEoin,
Lecturer in Islamic Studies,
Department of Religious Studies,
University of Newcastle Upon Tyne

Dr. Derek Hopwood,
University Lecturer in Modern Middle Eastern Studies,
Middle Eastern Bibliographer,
Fellow and Dean of St. Antony's College,
University of Oxford

Dr. Rodney Wilson,
Lecturer in the Economics of the Middle East,
Department of Economics,
University of Durham

Professor Miles Danby,
Professor of Architecture,
School of Architecture,
University of Newcastle Upon Tyne

INDEX

Index

147

Index